F-ing
inn◆vation

F-ing
inn✦vation

Why Innovation is Hard and
What to Do About it

Tamara Christensen

tamara@ideafarmcoop.com
ideafarmcoop.com

First Edition

Designed by Jennifer Duran
Hand Lettering by Tori Smith
Logo Design by Valerie Reynaud

For my son, my sun, Max

TABLE OF CONTENTS

WHY THIS BOOK

A few years ago I was asked to give a presentation about leadership to professionals in an Executive Master's program. I chose to talk about the challenges I see organizations face when they try to innovate. These challenges are a result of tensions related to knowledge, risk, assessment, pace of change, ambiguity and the playing field.

That presentation was the starting point of this book. It has since evolved into a framework I refer to as the "six tensions of transformation" and it involves many F words. Perhaps it's because I love discomfort and situations that make me think "What the F have I gotten myself into?" or maybe it's my love of alliteration. In any case, I chose to use F words to frame the opposing forces within each of these 6 tensions. And by F words I simply mean words that begin with the letter F. Nothing profane.

I also talked to that group about what it takes for a leader to transform tension into innovation: empathy, courage, evolutionary growth, experimentation, curiosity and connection. I believe that leadership is an act of facilitation, of making it easy for people to do their best work, so I call these characteristics "the innovation facilitator's mindset". Also— facilitation is one of my favorite F words.

I want to share with you a theory for understanding people and what makes us unique in our work. I know that our greatest strength, our most valuable asset to any effort we undertake, is exactly the thing that will drive someone else crazy. And yet we need each other. We need each other's diversity if we are going to successfully navigate the increasing complexity of business and work and collaboration.

It takes a village to solve a problem. It takes a wealth of diversity. And to solve big problems requires us to work together and bring the best of ourselves to the task at hand. So if I can offer one single thing to this constantly changing world that we live in I want to offer this one plea:

Please, let us change you.

Things changed a lot for me in 1987 when my parents divorced. I was in the 6th grade, already a time of big changes. My two younger siblings and I stayed with my father in the home in the small Kansas town where we had grown up.

My dad grew up in the Midwest, too. Nebraska. He liked to spend his down time fishing, tinkering in the garage and being outdoors. He had his own man cave/office in the basement where he would tie flies for fishing, load shot gun shells and work on a fancy new IBM computer.

I wanted nothing to do with the great outdoors. I covered my walls with collaged images cut from magazines, dressed like Madonna and choreographed dance routines to the latest hits in my bedroom. I spent my down time playing with the neighbor kids, imagining fantasy lands and inventing languages.

My dad was an engineer and a strict former military man who liked order and logic. I was the creative, emotional type who liked socializing and art and breaking rules. We experienced a lot of tension.

When I was in 7th grade I came home over-the-moon excited about a pink pleather skirt I had purchased that day at the mall. I put it on and showed my dad. He was clearly not happy about my choice. We fought about it and, like any good preteen would do, I yelled something disrespectful and stormed off to my room, slamming the door behind me.

A few hours later, an L.L. Bean catalog appeared on the floor inside my bedroom door. No doubt it had been slid under there by my dad. I gave it a quick once over, huffing dramatically on nearly every page. I couldn't believe my father thought I would want to dress like anyone in that dumb catalog!

But, truthfully, I was also touched by his effort. My father clearly had no sense of fashion. He didn't even like Madonna! But here he was, trying to connect with me, a 12-year-old girl, about clothing. He didn't know the words to say so he tried to communicate with something else.

I didn't change the way I dressed because of that interaction. In fact, I wore that skirt nearly every day. But I did change the way I thought about my dad.

In August of 2009, I started a new job as the Director of Research for an engineering and manufacturing firm. Originally a tooling and machine shop, the company had expanded over 40 years to include engineering, prototyping and, most recently, an in-house design group. This growth reflected a strategic move to "swim upstream" and offer creative services in the early stages of the package design process with the hopes of securing the tooling business.

I was finishing up graduate school in Arizona and searching for work in the midst of a pretty tough job market. I was excited to find a dream job doing what I loved in the Midwest. It was near where I grew up and still had family.

I was the most "upstream" hire to date and I felt like the "odd girl out" in many ways: One of only five women in a company of 300, one of only four people in the design group, the only person with academic and practical experience in design thinking, qualitative research and creative problem solving methods, the only person responsible for leading user research programs aimed at listening to the voice of the customer and translating that into value for design and engineering efforts, the only single mom.

On the very first day I sat down with Dave, the VP of Engineering who reminded me of my dad. He, too, was an engineer, an outdoorsman and hunter, easy going, super smart and incredibly systematic. After I filled out my paperwork and did some basic onboarding to company policies and procedures, Dave leaned forward across his desk. He smiled at me, held eye contact, and took a deep breath. Finally, he spoke.

D: Don't let us change you.

T: What do you mean?

D: I mean, we need you. We need this different way of thinking and doing things that you bring. It's why we hired you. And it's also why we will try to change you.

T: Um, okay...

D: We won't do it on purpose, but we won't be able to help ourselves. We do things a certain way around here and that won't be easy to change. So you are going to feel pushback and resistance and skepticism and all kinds of other things. I want you to be prepared for that.

T: I am prepared...I think.

D: Good. I want you to know that if you feel that, when you feel that way, that you are changing and there's too much pressure, you can come see me. Anytime.

T: Okay. I will. Come see you, I mean. Not change!

Little did I know, Dave was correct. I did change. A lot.

I leaned on Dave a lot to help me understand how to meet the needs of the engineers. I genuinely wanted to understand their ways of thinking and working. And Dave was committed to understanding the unusual needs and habits of the designers. We explored ways to bring out the best of both sides, to meet in the middle and expand each other's thinking.

It was a fun and challenging time that required me to stretch. I leveraged right brain creativity and left brain logic to honor different expertise and bring people together in productive collaboration. I earned the nickname "the glue" for my ability to facilitate engaging workshops between the designers and engineers and use consumer insights to unite their diverse perspectives on design requirements.

Even though the design group was tiny compared to the rest of the company, it felt as though we eventually created a sense of balance. We appreciated each other's differences and worked in ways that integrated diverse talent. It wasn't always easy, but we learned to value each other's strengths.

....

Please, let us change you.

By us I mean your peers, your managers, your employees, your competitors, your customers, your community, your family, even strangers. Please, oh please, let us change (even just a little, even for a few minutes) how you see the world.

Please be willing to consider an alternative point of view. Don't do it because you have to but because you want to and, perhaps most importantly, because you believe that our differences make us great and our capacity to navigate our tensions together will make the world a better place to work and live and thrive.

Dave, you were right. You did change me.

Fortunately, most everyone I have met has changed me in some way. And the more I learn about who I am (and who I am not) the more I appreciate the importance of collaboration.

A willingness to change flows from a willingness to learn. And I hope that you, dear reader, will learn something in this book that changes you, even if just a little, and transforms the way you feel about work.

"

Remember the
force will be with
you always.

"

Obi Wan
Kenobi

<u>WHY</u> IT IS SO HARD

Let's face it. Innovation isn't easy. We read about it business books and glossy articles and it looks so clean and fresh and clear. But those shiny outcomes don't always reveal the truth: innovation is hard work that requires us to roll up our sleeves and get our hands dirty with the people and processes that generate innovative outcomes.

Innovation

Change is inevitable, competition is fierce and challenges continue to get more complex. As Einstein so accurately pointed out, "We can't solve problems by using the same kind of thinking we used when we created them." Innovation often represents a new kind of thinking with the potential to help solve the problems of our rapidly changing world.

Innovation can be an elusive term so, to offer some context, when I speak about innovation in this book I am referring to the process of translating an idea or invention into something that creates value. Innovative solutions should be desired by customers or users (for novelty and/or functionality),

AN INNOVATION FRAMEWORK

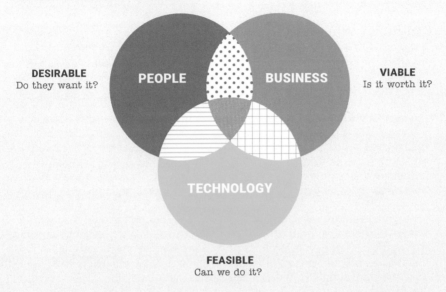

DESIRABLE
Do they want it?

PEOPLE

BUSINESS

VIABLE
Is it worth it?

TECHNOLOGY

FEASIBLE
Can we do it?

feasible in terms of technical capabilities and operations, and viable for both the customers and the business (a sound business model is possible).

And when I speak of innovation, I am also speaking about a human-centered approach to value creation. Humans are at the heart of all innovative solutions. People buy, make and manage innovation so it's important to engage people early and often throughout any process aimed at generating innovative outcomes.

Innovation efforts typically require organizations, teams and individuals to think and act in ways that feel unfamiliar and uncertain; ways that conflict with business-as-usual. In his classic 1969 book, Sciences of the Artificial, Herbert Simon wrote that "Everyone designs who devises courses of action aimed at changing existing situations into preferred ones." In essence, anyone seeking to innovate is designing the transformation from a current situation into an ideal one. This means that innovative leaders and changemakers are also transformation designers.

Crossing the chasm from an existing situation to a preferred one involves creative approaches to finding, framing and solving problems. These activities are sometimes collectively referred to as "design thinking." This approach describes a mindset that designers use as they move through different phases of activities: **Vision** (exploring possibilities, empathizing with people to see the world from their point of view), **Imagination** (framing problems to solve and experimenting with the iterative development of solutions) and **Activation** (implementing a plan and monitoring progress towards goals).

Transformation from existing to preferred rarely follows a rigid process or project path. So great design thinkers must also be great diagnosticians, adept at identifying when and how to move between different phases. Above all else, innovation requires a flexible approach that adapts and responds to the needs of the situation and the people impacted by it.

I think it is worth noting here that not all of the capabilities required to be a "designer" are necessary for the innovator or design thinker. There are many types of design: industrial, interior, interaction, graphic, architectural, etc. Each requires a set of technical or "hard skills" that are essential for producing the desired outcomes and complying with various regulations. Some design fields require licensure or certification and ongoing education.

This book is not intended to prepare designers for professional practice. Rather, it is aimed at preparing non-design professionals to practice applying the "soft skills" of design thinking when navigating innovation efforts. I hope it serves as a valuable tool for innovators to anticipate challenges, catalyze essential conversations and address issues that arise.

Are you an Innovator?

- Do you seek out alternative ways to approach challenges at work?
- Have you been asked to find a new solution to an enduring problem?
- Do you believe in the power of cross-functional collaboration?
- Are you curious about processes that are both creative and strategic?
- Do you resist the impulse to do things the same way they've always been done?
- Are you willing to champion a change in the status quo?

If you answered yes to any of the above, you just might be an innovator.

Innovation isn't the easiest of undertakings. Most innovators are fighting an uphill battle on multiple fronts within their organization. So, why do it? In some cases, there is no choice; leadership demands innovation and assesses performance against this requirement.

In other cases, innovative insurgents rise up within an organization, fueled by a strong desire to transform business-as-usual or disrupt the status quo.

Along the spectrum in between there are a variety of everyday innovators, catalyzing change for diverse reasons with varying levels of organizational permission and support.

Regardless of whether your motivations are extrinsic or intrinsic, there is great professional value in practicing innovation. You can develop skills to address challenges around growth, culture change, collaboration, engagement and leadership or team development. These experiences provide a strong foundation for creative leadership.

In a 2010 study by IBM, 60% of 1500 CEOs from around the globe listed creativity as the most important leadership trait for the future. Yes, the most important! More than integrity (52%) and global thinking (35%), creativity is considered essential for leaders who are wiling to depart from the status quo and value innovation as a catalyst for business growth. And there are lots of opportunities to practice being a creative problem solver.

Do any of these situations or innovators sound familiar?

Aaron is concerned that the culture in his organization is not conducive to collaboration or innovation (existing). He worries about attracting and retaining the talent required to prepare for the future of their industry (preferred). When asked to lead his company's strategic planning process, Aaron develops an inclusive and creative approach that engages employees across the organization. Aaron is an innovator.

Matt perceives a lack of appreciation between teams from different departments (existing) and fears that tenuous relationships are compromising everyone's ability to do their best work (preferred). He organizes cross-functional collaboration sessions to align different experts and foster a common understanding of customer needs. Matt is an innovator.

Fiona believes that people in other groups don't really understand what her staff does and why it is valuable (existing). She is concerned that teams don't know how to integrate the expertise they can provide (preferred). She develops a simple training program that introduces basic principles and tools that teams can immediately apply to their project. Fiona is an innovator.

Bill leads a talented team. He senses that the challenges they face with clients are due to miscommunication in early stages that result in a lack of strategic alignment (existing). He wants his team to develop stronger relationships with their clients (preferred) so he starts organizing workshops that provide frequent opportunities for people to convene in person, share ideas and clarify decisions. Bill is an innovator.

Stephanie is responsible for leadership development. She notices a communication gap between the newer, young leaders in the organization and senior leadership (existing). She wants future leaders to benefit from the wisdom and experience of those who are retiring (preferred) so she creates a game where pairs of junior/senior employees compete with each other to improve customer service. Stephanie is an innovator.

Maybe you have a story of your own based upon your role or responsibilities. Try this thought experiment:

1 Do you recognize any troubling or problematic elements in your current situation? Do you notice challenges in an existing project or team or work environment? If so, what are they?

2 What would improve the situation? Can you imagine a better version of the current reality? How would it be different? What is the preferred situation?

3 What would it take to make it happen? Can you think of some steps you could take to start moving towards a more preferable situation?

If that simple exercise got you to think about a better situation that you are prepared to pursue then you are an innovator.

This book is for innovators; people who are rolling up their sleeves and getting into the difficult and dirty work of transforming a current situation into an ideal one. It's for curious and courageous humans who believe in creative approaches but aren't quite sure what to expect or how to proceed.

This f-ing book prepares innovators for the difficult task of improving the experience for themselves and those around them. This book is about facilitating innovation and easing the tensions that it inevitably creates.

Innovation Creates Tension

Innovation is the process of translating an idea into something of value. It's fundamentally about getting from here (an existing situation that is not ideal) to there (a more preferred situation). This typically begins with awareness that the existing situation (or product or service or ratings, etc.) is not satisfactory for some reason.

There are plenty of inputs that signal a need to alter the status quo. Some examples include feedback from users, sales figures, employee surveys, and new competitors that disrupt the industry. Information can come in a variety of forms from both internal and external sources. Whatever the impetus, something happens and it becomes clear that something has to change. When change is afoot, people within organizations may resist new thinking and alternative approaches as they cling to what feels familiar and comfortable. "That's not how we do things here" or "There's no way we can get approval to do that" are artifacts of a mindset that stifles creative problem solving. Herein lies the challenge of being a creative leader because many innovation activities that are intended to bring value to the organization seem to run counter to usual practices.

Challenges that arise during innovation efforts typically signal an imbalance between two opposing forces: the usual and the unusual. I refer to these big influences as Business-As-Usual (BAU) and the Creativity Sustaining Atmosphere (CSA). BAU represents the prevailing paradigms of how things typically work in an organization- tradition, protocol and reliability. CSA represents an exploratory space where new ideas flourish and have the potential to grow into business value.

Both forces are essential and equally valuable. Neither is better or worse than the other. **The tension of transformation is a function of the distance and balance between two opposing forces in the midst of change.** The balance between the two forces signals the equilibrium of influence, i.e. more balance, more integrity. The span between the two forces signals the strength of each influence, i.e. greater span, greater impact.

BAU   CSA

Balance and distance generate the integrity and impact that lead to innovation breakthroughs. Imagine a rubber band being pulled in two opposite directions. When the opposing forces are strong, the rubber band stretches quite a bit and builds up a lot of potential energy. If, instead, the rubber band is pulled unevenly, it doesn't stretch uniformly and stores less potential energy.

BAU   CSA

If there is no tension, there is no potential energy. (boring)

BAU   CSA

If the span is too great, the rubber band stretches to the point of no return and breaks. (frustration)

BAU   CSA

WHY IT IS SO HARD

The goal is to also find the balance, to exert enough force on either side to stretch the rubber band so that, when released, that potential energy becomes energy in motion. This means making space for both ways of working, for really leaning into Business-As-Usual modes and tapping into that wellspring of expertise and success. It also means being equally influenced by the alternative; leaning into new and unfamiliar territory, a Creativity-Sustaining-Atmosphere, to explore possibilities and pave new paths forward.

The true task of an innovator is to balance the forces at play; i.e. to make it easy for everyone to bring the best elements of each force (and themselves) to the task at hand. This is important! It's not about prioritizing one way over the other, but finding a way to leverage the BEST OF BOTH.

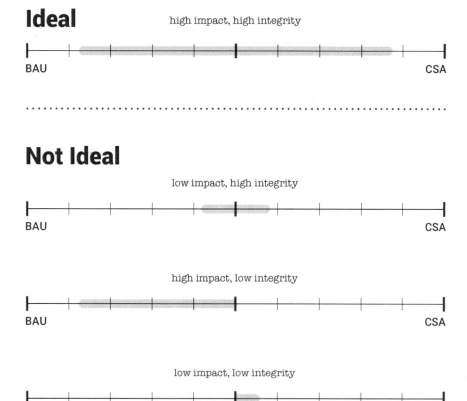

Ideal

high impact, high integrity

BAU   CSA

Not Ideal

low impact, high integrity

BAU   CSA

high impact, low integrity

BAU   CSA

low impact, low integrity

BAU   CSA

Impact represents the width of the bar and integrity represents how balanced the bar is.

A simple example is the tension between two team members: one creative and one technical. The creative is likely to be more influenced by imagining what is possible and what might be; whereas the technician is likely heavily influenced by facts about what exists and what can actually be done. Both are important, and both need equal influence if there is any hope of generating a truly innovative outcome.

If neither person is given the freedom to really bring their best thinking to the task, i.e. neither has much impact, then the outcome is likely to be boring or routine. If there is too much technical influence, the solution may lack creativity or desirability. If it's incredibly creative, it may be impossible to produce. In both cases there is a lack of integrity between the two areas of expertise. When both experts are given freedom to lean into their knowledge and put that potential in motion, there is a stronger likelihood for breakthrough innovation.

Tension is not a bad thing so long as we are able to stretch AND meet in the middle. Elasticity is essential for innovation- we want to have really strong forces that are equally powerful. Think of companies you admire: they are really strong at technical AND creative, engineering AND design, function AND form, strategy AND tactics, what's possible AND what's desirable. We need both and we need balance.

Helping others to innovate begins with understanding why it feels so f-ing hard in the first place. Most challenges that arise during innovation efforts are a result of tension between competing forces that are imbalanced. Facilitating innovation means to ease the tensions of transformation.

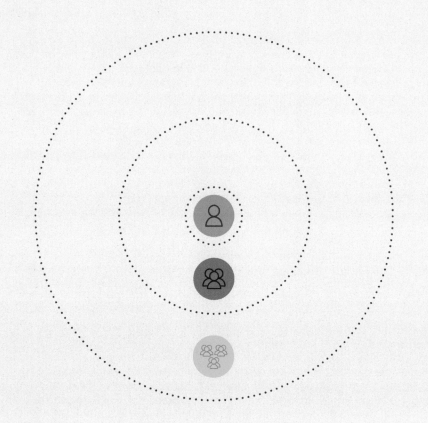

INDIVIDUAL MINDSET
The internal thoughts, preferences, values and habits of an individual that shape personal thoughts, actions and decision making.

GROUP/TEAM MINDSET
The collective preferences, values and habits of a group or team that shape group thinking, collaborative efforts and decision making.

ORGANIZATIONAL CULTURE
The collective and prevailing beliefs, values, processes, etc. of an organization that shape strategy, operations and decision making.

Tension is Systemic

Before exploring the tensions, it's important to recognize their systemic nature. What happens within an organization is a reflection of what happens within the different groups and individuals within the system. They all impact and influence each other.

Mindset exists at an individual level and may also operate at a team or department level. The collective mindset of an organization is the culture; the beliefs, values, attitudes, hierarchies, processes, norms and habits that make up business-as-usual.

Culture describes an organizational climate that is experienced everyday by people, in conversations and meetings and even in moments alone in front of their computer. Reciprocally, what happens with individual workers and teams shapes the culture. The elements of culture are interdependent and continuously cocreated by all of the stakeholders in the system.

As we take a deeper look at these tensions, consider them within the context of this system. Consider yourself and your own preferences and style as a leader and colleague. Consider the different teams and projects you work with as well as your business unit or department. And consider your entire organization and the norms that characterize your culture.

It is possible (and even likely) that there are both similarities and differences in how each level of the system experiences the tensions. Similarities may go unnoticed as they are rarely disruptive. Discrepancies, however, reveal the forces at play that impact innovation efforts. They may provide some insight into how to understand and overcome various challenges that emerge.

The 6 Tensions of Transformation

Over the past 15 years I have led a variety of innovation efforts for diverse organizations, from small local not-for-profits to global Fortune 100 corporations. Through these experiences I identified six common obstacles that arise when individuals, teams and organizations prioritize innovation and begin to experiment with new approaches that disrupt the status quo.

A LACK OF COMPELLING DATA: We are most comfortable with the way we are doing things and aren't likely to change up the status quo without a compelling reason to try something new. What constitutes a "compelling reason" varies greatly and is influenced by how an organization prioritizes different types of information.

A FEAR OF CHANGE: We want to be innovative, so long as we don't have to change too much, i.e. we often don't know how to go about it because we are used to doing things a certain way. Change can be scary and this fear stalwarts efforts to try something new, simply because it's different.

A FEAR OF FAILURE: We are unsure of how to begin and, most importantly, afraid to fail if we try. Projects are identified as successes or failures and failure stories are used as mythical warnings of what not to do.

ANALYSIS PARALYSIS: We are either overwhelmed with data or don't have enough of it. In either case, we become paralyzed with indecision and incapable of making meaningful progress towards innovation goals.

DISCOMFORT WITH UNCERTAINTY: Our current best practices don't tolerate a high level of risk or ambiguity. We want a plan we can execute with a high degree of certainty, and prefer to proceed with a clear path forward.

REACTION TO COMPETITION: We live in a world where competition is king and we spend more time being reactive than strategic. Most of our initiatives are undertaken as defensive efforts to stay ahead of the competition. We are playing to win.

These challenges reveal where resistance shows up across six tensions of transformation. We must begin with an understanding of where the tensions originate. Then we can understand how to remedy the imbalances of opposing forces and promote the kind of productive, creative tension that fuels innovation.

So what are the big challenges that make it feel so hard for committed, creative leaders to implement innovation efforts within their organizations and teams?

KNOWLEDGE: What constitutes knowledge used for decision making, including how information is generated, communicated and prioritized in order to make it actionable.

RISK: Orientation to vulnerability and exposure to potential loss, including the degree of willingness to try something new without certainty of outcomes.

ASSESSMENT: How efforts and outcomes are measured; belief that what is measured will grow. Ability to learn from experience and transfer learning to others.

PACE OF CHANGE: The rate of speed at which elements of a system can undergo change and adaptation given the information that is available at the time.

AMBIGUITY: Tolerance for uncertainty and willingness to proceed with a plan that is likely to change during the course of implementation.

PLAYING FIELD: Understanding key stakeholders who impact and are impacted, awareness of context and landscape that shapes decision making.

Knowledge

BAU ⊢——┼——┼——┼——┼——┼——┼——┼——┼——┼——⊣ CSA

FACTS   FEELINGS

Risk

BAU ⊢——┼——┼——┼——┼——┼——┼——┼——┼——┼——⊣ CSA

FEAR   FAITH

Assessment

BAU ⊢——┼——┼——┼——┼——┼——┼——┼——┼——┼——⊣ CSA

FAILURE   FUEL

Pace of Change

BAU ⊢——┼——┼——┼——┼——┼——┼——┼——┼——┼——⊣ CSA

FROZEN   FAST

Ambiguity

BAU ⊢——┼——┼——┼——┼——┼——┼——┼——┼——┼——⊣ CSA

FAMILIAR   FOREIGN

Playing Field

BAU ⊢——┼——┼——┼——┼——┼——┼——┼——┼——┼——⊣ CSA

FIERCE   FRIENDS

In the sections that follow I'll describe these tensions in more detail. For each tension, we'll explore the opposing forces and why they are both valuable. We'll also explore what it looks like when there is an imbalance and one force is exerting more influence than the other. You will have the opportunity to apply what you are learning as you assess yourself, your team and your organization. Finally, reflect on what the assessment reveals to you and explore new ways of thinking about collaboration.

NO.

01

KNOWLEDGE

How to Know?

What constitutes knowledge used for decision making, including how information is generated, communicated and prioritized in order to make it actionable.

In Business-As-Usual, most decisions are fact-based and focus on the "what". Something is considered knowable (and valuable) if it can be presented through numerically-based forms including percentages, charts, graphs, tables, etc. There is comfort and safety in numbers and a belief that numbers represent truth. Analytics play a significant role in fueling the identification of opportunities and the evaluation of solutions.

In a Creativity Sustaining Atmosphere, feelings and emotional experience are key drivers when making decisions and emphasize the "why" and "how". In a CSA it is important to consider the feelings of people who have a stake in an opportunity or challenge. This may include customers, of course, but also other individuals within an entire process or system that brings a solution to life including people within different business units, retailers, wholesalers, customer-facing personnel, and other staff who support delivery.

"

Human behavior
flows from
3 main sources:
desire, emotion
& knowledge.

Plato "

Facts

Prioritizing information about what has happened, is happening or might happen that is easily translated into numeric, quantifiable form for manipulation and representation during opportunity identification and decision making.

∙∙∙

Data is a tool for understanding and making decisions. Data is used in business to document what has happened, what is currently happening and what may happen in the future. The more facts we have about a situation (a product or service or market or trend, etc.) the more confident we feel about making decisions that are based on that information.

These days, the internet (including sources like Google and Wikipedia) makes it possible, and even easy, to answer any question that we have.

Thanks to "big data" we can now answer really big questions and explore trends and patterns across large sample populations. Never before in history have we had so much data available to collect and analyze.

Organizations rely on data, and more specifically facts, to improve decision making and reduce risk. Unfortunately facts don't tell the whole story so they aren't reliable as the only indicator of the past, the present or the potential.

Feelings

Prioritizing information about the human experience, including how it is processed internally and the beliefs, values and thoughts that influence choices during opportunity identification and decision making.

Facts will tell you WHAT you want to know (how many people do x, how many times per day they do x and which brand they prefer to use for x) but these numerical figures will never be able to tell you WHY, the feelings that fuel those choices about x. And folks, feelings matter.

Using various sources of data (i.e. both facts AND feelings) enables you to tap into emotional elements that impact how and why people do what they do. This combination of information is valuable for evaluating current or past situations and for generating future opportunities by identifying problems or dissatisfaction. It is increasingly clear that how people experience a product or service matters just as much as (or more than) the simple functionality. To surprise and delight humans, you must embrace emotion.

Leaders from a state Department of Fish & Wildlife (DFW) were facing a mandatory price increase for hunting and fishing licenses and permits. Typically, when required to raise prices, the agency is tasked with figuring out how to do it, and justify it, in a way that doesn't upset their constituents too much. There is no choice- the prices must go up. And there is no denying that price hikes can cause tension for customers.

Although the DFW had no choice but to raise prices, they did have a choice about how they could engage people in a conversation about why the prices were going up. In the past, and in other states, this is achieved with statewide surveys that generate Facts and analytics about which fee increases might generate the least resistance. The conversation is often focused on WHAT combination of fee hikes people are most likely to accept (or least likely to resist).

We helped the DFW reframe the opportunity to include WHY people purchased licenses and permits and how they would prefer to do it.

We also wanted to explore which elements of the experience to improve.

Instead of looking solely at the facts, the DFW decided to conduct informal focus groups around the state. They asked various constituents to share needs and ideas for improving the license and permitting process. They listened to how people felt about the process and where they felt the most friction or disappointment.

Insights from these conversations became fuel for an innovation session that I designed and facilitated. Participants included DFW leaders and representatives from diverse groups around the state. They all worked together to generate new ideas to improve the value of the licenses and permits, many of which were relatively easy for the DFW to implement and inexpensive to achieve. The most promising ideas were then included in the statewide survey to determine if they had broad appeal.

The DFW recognized that people tend to be unhappy about a price hike. They could have focused solely on using facts to make price hikes tolerable (a BAU approach). Instead, they recognized the value of listening to people and asking about their experience and ideas- to consider feelings and desires (a CSA approach).

By balancing the tension of knowledge, the DFW was able to identify innovative ways to improve the value of the license and permit experience and create a preferred situation that satisfies the needs of multiple stakeholders.

What does it look
and feel like when an
organization, team or
individual is heavily
influenced by one
opposing force?

Facts or Feelings

FACTS   FEELINGS

Too Much Facts

An organization that succumbs to the allure of Facts may be overly
dependent upon quantitative data and rely heavily upon charts, graphs
and statistical modeling for decision making. There may also be general
skepticism about any information that cannot be presented in this manner
or a complete rejection of more qualitative types of data. Employees may
feel disengaged or disempowered to change the situation without exhaustive
efforts to collect and communicate significant findings. Customers may feel
skeptical about the organizations' commitment to their personal experience
and question brand loyalty.

Fact-focused teams may unintentionally alienate members or miss
opportunities for breakthrough ideas. Individuals who lean towards Facts
may struggle to influence decisions or build strong cross-functional
relationships. These teams may also lack trust and a sense of cohesion if an
emphasis is placed solely on the tasks at hand without regard for individual
expertise and experience.

An individual who focuses primarily on the Facts prioritizes logical and
analytical approaches to problem solving and often drives toward a
solution. S/he may avoid exploration of the softer, human side of a situation
and rely exclusively on observable data when making decisions. Too much
emphasis on facts may result in missed opportunities to explore nuance
and complexity of a challenge and potentially reduce the ability to generate
novel solutions.

FACTS   FEELINGS

Too Much Feelings

An organization that succumbs to the gravitational pull of Feelings may rely more upon hunches and instincts than data. It may place too much emphasis on every piece of customer or employee feedback, resulting in quick, reactionary decisions that divert from strategic goals. Employees may feel like they are in a race to keep up with the latest and greatest trend or visionary whim of leadership. Customers may feel confused about the organization's brand and uncertain about it's ability to consistently deliver quality products or services for the long term.

Teams that are overly influenced by Feelings may struggle to have difficult conversations out of fear of conflict. On the contrary, there may too much conflict based upon emotional triggers rather than factual information. Choices and priorities may be based more on intuition and assumption than data which makes it difficult to arrive at a rational, logical decision.

An individual who over prioritizes Feelings may lose sight of the bigger picture (i.e. more focus on the internal experience than the external context and factors). This emphasis on Feelings can lead to a narrow perception of a challenge, a reluctance to consider conflicting information (be it evidence or emotion) and difficulties communicating choices with others who prefer a logical case for making a decision.

KNOWLEDGE

Assessment Using the Scales

Use the scale to assess the tension between these two opposing forces of Facts and Feelings. Place a mark on each side of the scale, one for each force. The closer the mark is to either end of the spectrum, the stronger the pull. The closer to the center the mark is, the less force is exerted by that side.

This is not an "either/or" choice, rather you will indicate the strength of each force on both sides and then connect these marks to create a bar that illustrates the tension between the two. The wider the bar, the stronger the tension (both forces exerting strong influence), while a shorter bar represents less tension (neither force exerting strong influence). The goal is balance and, ideally, a wider bar. A shorter bar often indicates that there is not enough of either force to produce the kind of creative tension necessary for truly breakthrough innovation.

Consider how you, your team and your organization orient to knowledge. What type of knowledge do you consider valid, reliable, essential, or representative of the "truth"? For each of the following scales representing elements of the system, indicate the strength of the pull of Facts by placing a mark on the left side. Indicate the strength of the pull of Feelings by placing a mark on the right side. Once you have marks on either side, connect them to create a bar that demonstrates the width and location along the scale.

You. Consider yourself first. When faced with a challenge or opportunity, what kind of knowledge do you seek and prioritize? What kind of inputs do you require to feel confident about how to proceed?

high   low   high

FACTS   FEELINGS

Your team. Pick a team or group of people that you work with and consider how, in general, the team prioritizes different inputs of knowledge. When faced with a challenge or opportunity, what kind of knowledge do you seek and prioritize? What kind of inputs do you require to feel confident about how to proceed? What kinds of conversations do you have when making decisions? What kinds of conversation are off limits?

high   low   high

FACTS   FEELINGS

Your organization. Now think about your organization as a whole. When faced with a challenge or opportunity, what kind of knowledge does the organization seek and prioritize? What kinds of inputs are required to generate confidence about how to proceed? What kinds of conversations happen about how and why decisions are made and the information used to make them? What kinds of conversation are off limits?

high   low   high

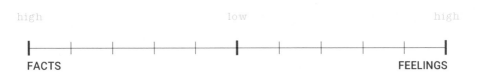

FACTS   FEELINGS

Reflection

○ What do you notice about your assessments?

○ Which force is exerting the most impact?

○ Where do you see the most (or least) balance? Is there integrity?

○ Are there strong similarities or differences across the three scales?

○ How might you use this scale to understand other stakeholders (i.e. team member, client, leader, etc.)?

NO.
02

RISK

What's at Stake?

Orientation to vulnerability and exposure to potential loss, including the degree of willingness to try something new without certainty of outcomes.

Business-As-Usual is often fueled by fear: fear of change, fear of the unknown, fear of competition, fear of loss, fear of uncertainty, fear of repercussions, etc. These fears may be justified and typically live on within the organization because they have generated favorable outcomes, namely increase in revenue and growth. Risk aversion is considered a cornerstone of business growth because it prevents catastrophic errors and losses. Fear of risk plays a significant role in the assessment of opportunities and how resources are allocated towards potential solutions and initiatives.

In a Creativity Sustaining Atmosphere, risk is considered a healthy part of the innovation process. The presence of fear signals an opportunity for growth, either in overcoming an obstacle or heading in a new direction (i.e. fight or flight). Innovation challenges are often wicked problems; i.e. solving one problem yields new, unintended consequences and additional problems to solve. It is impossible to predict every potential scenario. Pursuing innovation therefore requires awareness of risks as they emerge and faith that, no mater what comes up, it is always possible to generate a solution that can serve multiple stakeholders.

" I learned that courage was not the absence of fear, but the triumph over it. The brave is not he who does not feel afraid, but he who conquers that fear. **"**

Nelson Mandela

An unwillingness to act due to a belief that something is dangerous or threatening; risk aversion during opportunity identification and decision making.

· ·

A young child waits at the gate with his parents to embark on his very first plane ride. He is visibly excited and bursting with energy; bouncing around, fidgeting, yelling, crying, trying to run off, etc. The mother leans over and wraps her arm around the child's shoulder. "There there, honey," she says soothingly into his ear, "don't be afraid." He calms down.

Two critical things happened during that exchange. First, the child learned to label the feeling of anticipation that he was experiencing as "fear". Secondly, he learned that he should stop feeling

it. Mom said not to feel that so he learned to suppress it. He learned that it has a name and that it evokes shame. Yikes.

This little tale illustrates how even the best of intentions (by parents and businesses) can produce unintended outcomes. In the story, a mom's effort to calm her child leads to an association between a feeling and an undesirable label. The sensation that many of us identify as a thing called "fear" is merely excitement for the unknown. Fear itself is not wrong. The problem lies in how we respond to

Faith

A willingness to try something new where there exists no proof or certainty of a successful outcome; risk affection during opportunity identification and decision making.

. . . .

that feeling. We have been taught (explicitly and implicitly, intentionally and unintentionally) to avoid that feeling, to run in the other direction when it comes up; to suppress the enthusiasm and assume it signals impending danger. We have learned to flee from fear rather than face it and embrace it.

Yes, we are afraid of being innovative. Why? Because it's new! We don't know exactly what will happen! There's so much to lose. But there is also much to gain.

Innovation involves ambiguity and uncertainty. It involves taking risks, being brave, and having the courage to try something different. When we try something new we are facing the unknown. We have to acknowledge our fears and then put them to the side so that we can move forward with caution and confidence, with faith that we can handle whatever comes our way.

We were approached by a leader in the Strategy group of a water and power utility who was looking for innovative ways to rethink strategic planning. The standard strategic planning process involved leaders at the very highest levels of the organization who chart the course and outline key initiatives, etc. In the past, various attempts had been made to translate high-level strategic objectives into more meaningful goals for employees across the company yet people still complained that they felt disconnected from the strategic plan and were unclear about how their daily efforts directly impacted the company's goals.

Strategic planning for Business-As-Usual is typically carried out by an exclusive group of leaders who set the course for the company's future. This elite team is responsible for conducting SWOT analyses, exploring forecasts and trends and identifying ways to mitigate risk in pursuit of growth. The outcomes of these activities include goals and initiatives that must be implemented by others.

But one enlightened leader felt that many of the downstream challenges of implementing a strategic plan could be solved through an innovative approach to creating the plan itself. We designed a program that engaged employees across the organization in an iterative process of generating information to influence the most senior leadership in their strategic planning efforts.

We began with a team of carefully chosen Catalysts, mid-level and high potential young leaders from across the different business units, who were tasked to create the SWOT (Strengths, Weaknesses, Opportunities, Threats) analysis. We trained these Catalysts in creative problem finding, framing and solving methods and facilitated their efforts.

They created a provocative synthesis of information and presented it in a narrative and visual style that captivated leadership and set a new standard within the company.

As the strategic planning process evolved and moved into higher levels of leadership, the Catalysts continued to participate and became a trusted source of inspiration and input. While we originally called this program

"Strategy Cocreation", it was often referred to internally as the "bottom up" approach to strategic planning. In many ways, it did turn the organization upside down.

A Business-As-Usual approach would have succumbed to entrenched fears about who should be responsible for strategy and how decisions that shape the future of the company should be made. Instead, this company cultivated a Creativity Sustaining Atmosphere that engaged employees in rich conversations about the future. In fact, one of the key insights from the Catalyst efforts was about culture and the detrimental force that fear and mistrust asserted in the work environment. Addressing these cultural challenges is now part of the strategic plan.

This organization recognized that a standard (BAU) approach to strategic planning would likely produce familiar results and deepen the feelings of disconnection between employees, leaders and organizational objectives. Instead, they took a risk and faced their fears about how to prepare for the future.

They believed that if they balanced this fear with faith and engaged many voices in the conversation that they would be better prepared to face the complex landscape of their industry together. In so doing they generated new ways to frame challenges and innovative approaches to overcome them. And, perhaps most importantly, they courageously changed the conversation about what it means for an organization to craft and implement a strategic plan that meets the needs and leverages the strengths of diverse stakeholders.

What does it look and feel like when an organization, team or individual is heavily influenced by one *opposing force?*

FEAR   FAITH

Too Much Fear

An organization that is dominated by Fear is plagued by a lack of trust among its people and may be perceived as stagnant or lagging in the marketplace. The more fear present in an organization, the less trust. Trust is key for fostering engagement and innovation. When people in an organization fear speaking out against prevailing ways of thinking, they bring less and less of themselves to their work and eventually disengage. This leads to dysfunction among various groups where people are unwilling or unmotivated to have difficult conversations or challenge authority.

The more an organization fears risk, the less capable it is to foster commitment, productivity and potential for innovation. Fear-dominated organizations may have tenuous relationships with vendors and customers if they are reluctant to receive honest feedback or actively address issues that arise. They may also mitigate risk by avoiding it and requiring their customers or other stakeholders to assume risk they are unwilling to face.

Teams that are plagued by Fear are characterized by a lack of productivity, poor performance, and misalignment. Decreased productivity is often the result of mistrust of team members and others who influence team activities. This creates a team culture where people are afraid to speak openly about the challenges and opportunities they see because they fear the repercussions of conflict. When Fear is present and engagement is low, team performance is reduced because people don't bring the best of themselves to their tasks. When team members aren't trusting or engaged, they aren't able to get aligned on collaborative efforts and move forward as a cohesive unit.

A Fear-focused Individual is likely unwilling to speak openly about ideas or challenges because they are afraid of the backlash. This lack of trust in leadership and peers often results in "behind closed doors" conversations or suggestions made "off the record." Sadly, these folks often have valuable contributions but are unwilling to risk putting themselves (or their job) on the line by speaking up. So they endure the status quo and keep their gifts to themselves. Too much Fear can cause burnout, i.e. when the employee won't risk saying no, and active disengagement, i.e. when fear builds up over time and someone passively retaliates by trying to undermine people and projects.

FEAR   FAITH

Too Much Faith

An organization that is influenced heavily by Faith has little concern for risk and may pursue ideas and opportunities without careful consideration of potential consequences. These organizations are characterized by rapid response to industry and market trends and quick pivots in strategic directions. This may result in feelings of insecurity about work, performance and value for employees who are trying to keep up with constant shifts and long for clarity about where things are headed. Customers may find it difficult to remain loyal to a brand that is in constant flux, chasing down the latest flavor of the month/year/etc. and mitigating the costs of overly risky ventures.

An overly Faithful team may have little to no Fear about the consequences of their efforts and therefore be perceived as disconnected from the organization and even renegade in their approach. These groups are comfortable embracing risk, whatever the cost, and may resist input or guidance from outside sources with more awareness of organizational history, industry trends or macro forces at play. This overconfidence can alienate valuable entities and foster feelings of resentment for efforts that appear more tactical than strategic. Teams heavily influenced by the force of Faith may have a more short-sighted or myopic view of their efforts within the context of the entire organization.

When an individual is dominated by Faith and refuses to acknowledge the Fear associated with risk, s/he may be perceived as cavalier, maverick or even dangerous. Visionary leaders, for example, may sometimes appear to be guided by an intuitive Faith and belief in their goals, especially when they act alone or resist consult from others. When one refuses to consider the many variables within a situation, this negligence can lead to dire consequences. Without fear or consideration of consequences, risk affection may cost an individual the respect of peers, the trust and progress of teams, and the potential for advancement within the organization.

Assessment Using the Scales

Use the scale to assess the tension between these two opposing forces of Fear and Faith. Place a mark on each side of the scale, one for each force. The closer the mark is to either end of the spectrum, the stronger the pull. The closer to the center the mark is, the less force is exerted by that side.

This is not an "either/or" choice, rather you will indicate the strength of each force on both sides and then connect these marks to create a bar that illustrates the tension between the two. The wider the bar, the stronger the tension (both forces exerting strong influence), while a shorter bar represents less tension (neither force exerting strong influence). The goal is balance and, ideally, a wider bar. A shorter bar often indicates that there is not enough of either force to produce the kind of creative tension necessary for truly breakthrough innovation.

Consider how you, your team and your organization orient to risk. When confronted with risk, how do you respond? For each of the following scales representing elements of the system, indicate the strength of the pull of Fear by placing a mark on the left side. Indicate the strength of the pull of Faith by placing a mark on the right side. Once you have marks on either side, connect them to create a bar that demonstrates the width and location along the scale.

You. Consider yourself first. When faced with risk, how do you feel? Are you excited by the challenge and prepared to face it head on? How do you communicate with others about risk and respond to their concerns?

high   low   high

FEAR   FAITH

Your team. Pick a team that you work with and consider how, in general, the team responds to risk. Do you embrace the opportunity to try something new and plan to mitigate risk? How do you communicate about the risk involved? How does risk impact the efforts and decisions of the team? How is team performance impacted during risky situations?

high   low   high

FEAR   FAITH

Your organization. Now think about your organization as a whole. When faced with a challenge or opportunity, how does the organization respond to risk? How does potential risk impact the overall culture and environment of decision making? How does risk impact strategic planning and organizational communication?

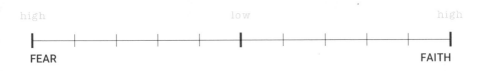

high   low   high

FEAR   FAITH

Reflection

○ What do you notice about your assessments?

○ Which force is exerting the most impact?

○ Where do you see the most (or least) balance? Is there integrity?

○ Are there strong similarities or differences across the three scales?

○ How might you use this scale to understand other stakeholders (i.e. team member, client, leader, etc.)?

NO.

03

ASSESSMENT

What to Measure?

How efforts and outcomes are measured; belief that what is measured will grow. Ability to learn from experience and transfer learning to others.

Business-As-Usual tends to foster a fixed mindset where a clearly defined outcome is the objective for a strategic pursuit. Anything less than goal achievement is often deemed a failure. Goals and success metrics are identified and committed to and then used to benchmark progress and performance. This focus on products of our efforts creates a polarizing paradigm where not achieving successful equates to failure. A fixed mindset can also represent a belief that talents are innate and capabilities are pretty limited.

A growth mindset recognizes that even when we don't achieve a specific outcome, we still benefit from the experience of trying. This means there are plenty of opportunities to learn and develop, even in the face of our worst "failures". In a Creativity Sustaining Atmosphere, it is essential to recognize that when we are "failing" to meet goals, we are learning. **When we are learning, we are nearling** — getting closer to a more complete and accurate picture of success and pushing into new, nearby territory of skill development.

66

Failures, repeated
failures are finger
posts on the road
to achievement.
One fails forward
to success.

C.S. Lewis

99

A fixed mindset that uses a success/failure paradigm when identifying opportunities and making decisions.

. . . .

We often set out with a goal or target in mind. Maybe it's a sales quota, a customer satisfaction score, employee engagement ratings or brand recognition. We have goals that are quantitative (and numeric) and goals that are qualitative (experiential).

Business-as-Usual relies upon goals and metrics to assess progress. Goals are good, but measuring ourselves- and our work- only by how well we meet these goals is not good and it won't promote a Creativity Sustaining Atmosphere. Here's why: We set goals with a limited amount of information in an effort to predict

an ideal outcome, but we can never really know what will happen until we are in the thick of it. That's why it's also important to learn as we go and identify new ways to assess progress during our efforts.

Yes, in the middle of the work, we may need to find new goals. As we implement a project plan, we will undoubtedly face things that we didn't expect, i.e. the unintended consequences of our efforts. What emerges may help or hinder our progress. And these events can force us to think differently about our objectives.

Fuel

A growth mindset that considers the learning value
of activities related to identifying opportunities and
making decisions.

As we "fail" to meet original goals, we learn something new about the nature of the challenge and how to address it. We get a little closer to really delivering on the best possible outcome. When things don't go exactly as we had planned or hoped (and they rarely do), we don't have to consider it failure.

Instead, we can frame these learning lessons as nearlings, important evidence that we are getting better at understanding what we want to achieve and getting closer to making the ideal a reality. We don't want to feel like we have wasted time and efforts if things emerge a bit differently than we planned, so the key is to approach these unexpected insights as learning opportunities and find a way to make them valuable. As we reflect on these experiences, we can apply our insights to our future efforts.

Nearly a year had passed since the launch of a major internal innovation training initiative so our client, a Fortune 100 corporation with 150,000 employees in 150 countries, wanted to take stock and assess the impact of the program so far. We were asked to conduct a post-training study with a sample of program participants and their managers to understand how participants were applying their learning in the context of daily work.

Around this time we were also designing a continuing education offering and train-the-trainer program to meet international demand for more workshops. Our goals for the study were to benchmark progress, collect success stories, identify potential trainees, and validate our hypotheses about the value of the new tools we hoped to include in the continuing education program.

Truthfully, we expected our interviews with past participants would yield many stories of triumph. We did hear successful case studies, but we also heard a lot of frustration. Although they wanted to apply their learning, many employees were struggling with translating tools to their specific work challenges. They felt like they had failed to use every tool in the right way and hence questioned their own aptitude.

Additionally, we heard that trainees had difficult communicating about the value of the new tools with their colleagues. More importantly, they struggled get aligned with their managers about how to assess their efforts and establish appropriate performance metrics. We hadn't truly prepared them to address these challenges.

In a Business-As-Usual world, we might have interpreted the data as a sign of failure, of not meeting all of the program goals for getting employees to apply and integrate the new approach.

Instead, we chose to frame the feedback as fuel for improvement and dove in deeper to better understand what these employees and their managers truly needed.

We chose to address these needs and foster a Creativity Sustaining Atmosphere. We reframed our initial continuing education goals to focus more on meeting the immediate needs of participants and their leaders.

We reprioritized our original goal introduce a whole new set of tools. Instead we developed a kit of materials for managers to help prepare them to support their employees before, during and after the training experience.

We also created a capabilities "rubric" for assessing behaviors that could be used by both trainees and their managers. Finally, we designed smaller interventions to integrate during the training that helped maintain connections between participants and their bosses and fostered more communication about the value of the new learning.
We also identified potential trainers and engaged them in our process of improving the original training to ensure that it had staying power.

We set out with clear goals for our initiative and we were willing to listen generously to the feedback of key stakeholders. Rather than sticking to a rigid definition of success and failure, we embraced a growth mindset and acknowledged the potential of new insights to reframe our objectives. We paid close attention to where people felt like they (and we) were "failing" and leveraged this learning to create new opportunities for improving the program and help people make decisions about the way that the organization assesses innovation performance.

What does it look and feel like when an organization, team or individual is heavily influenced by one *opposing force?*

FAILURE   FUEL

Too Much Failure

When an organization is dominated by a Failure force, it often shows up in the internal processes that guide progress and development through rigid metrics and rigorous stage/gate programs. Failure paradigms set up a "go or no go" framework where effort and outcomes either pass or fail. It is a black and white world where things are either right or wrong and no one wants to be wrong. When everyone wants to be "right" there is increased internal competition and judgment that inhibits collaboration and a spirit of learning from experience. From the outside, these organizations may be perceived as difficult to work with and incapable of adapting to client and customer needs.

Teams that are heavily influenced by the force of Failure are likely inhibited by past successes and failures. Team members may use stories from previous efforts to shape opportunity identification and decision making activities, i.e. "that's already been explored" or "they tried that last year and failed" or "this worked before so let's do it that way again". In high stakes situations, where pressure to perform and deliver is high, these groups can experience extreme stress about getting it right the first time. This force compromises collaboration because individuals within the team may suffer from intensely competitive relationships due to a strong need for "credit" when things go right or, conversely, may resist deep engagement for fear of being held accountable when things are deemed to have gone wrong.

If an Individual is pulled by the force of Failure and believes strongly in the polarity of success and failure, they may exhibit a strong need to control situations in order to avoid mistakes. Though they often have the best of intentions, these individuals may be overly critical of themselves and others in their pursuit of the successful outcome. Employees who exhibit a fixed-mindset can be incredibly hard on themselves for poor performance, may feel shame or a sense of unworthiness, and question their ability to develop their skills and capabilities.

FAILURE   FUEL

Too Much Fuel

When an organization is overpowered by a growth mindset and promotes a cultural belief that all experiences can generate Fuel for learning, this may be accompanied by a lack of clearly articulated strategic goals that employees can reference and align their actions to. When Fuel forces are strong, anything is fodder for learning and nothing is inherently right or wrong so it becomes difficult to assess progress and performance. Additionally, when an organization has no clear system for tracking progress towards goals, it may lack focus and become too divergent- shifting direction based upon the outcomes of every effort.

When Fuel is the primary force of a team it may be difficult to complete work and deliver outcomes because every effort yields new information that opens up new potential for another iteration of the outcome, only this time even better! These groups lack adherence to stated goals and objectives, or prefer to disregard them completely as they respond to new data and feedback about their efforts. Instead of driving towards objectives, these teams meander in various directions and organically progress towards a target that is constantly on the move. When there is no clear sense of right and wrong, team members may struggle to situate themselves as a valuable member of the team and blur boundaries between different roles and tasks.

When an individual is dominated by a growth mindset and pulled by the force of Fuel, they enjoy a lifelong learning approach that generates lessons from every experience, often to their own detriment. If anything is valuable, then everything is valuable and it becomes hard to sort through the possibilities and identify clear goals. During collaboration these individuals may frustrate others because they refuse to concede the success or failure of anything and have difficulty using criteria to assess the merit of an idea or decision. Fuel-force folks may also appear arrogant or overly confident because they are immune to fear of failure.

Assessment Using the Scales

Use the scale to assess the tension between these two opposing forces of Failure and Fuel. Place a mark on each side of the scale, one for each force. The closer the mark is to either end of the spectrum, the stronger the pull. The closer to the center the mark is, the less force is exerted by that side.

This is not an "either/or" choice, rather you will indicate the strength of each force on both sides and then connect these marks to create a bar that illustrates the tension between the two. The wider the bar, the stronger the tension (both forces exerting strong influence), while a shorter bar represents less tension (neither force exerting strong influence). The goal is balance and, ideally, a wider bar. A shorter bar often indicates that there is not enough of either force to produce the kind of creative tension necessary for truly breakthrough innovation.

Consider how you, your team and your organization orient to assessment. What is measured and how is it communicated (formally and informally)? For each of the following scales representing elements of the system, indicate the strength of the pull of Failure by placing a mark on the left side. Indicate the strength of the pull of Fuel by placing a mark on the right side. Once you have marks on either side, connect them to create a bar that demonstrates the width and location along the scale.

You. Consider yourself first. When faced with a challenge or opportunity, how do you assess the potential? How do you respond when your efforts produce less than favorable results or unintended consequences?

high   low   high

FAILURE   FUEL

Your team. Pick a team that you work with and consider how, in general the team approaches assessment. When faced with a challenge or opportunity, how do you assess the potential? How do you respond when your efforts produce less than favorable results or unintended consequences? How do you communicate about progress towards goals? How do you share the work and acknowledge contributions?

high   low   high

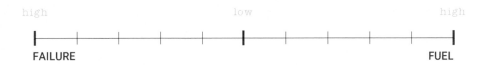

FAILURE   FUEL

Your organization. Now think about your organization as a whole. When faced with a challenge or opportunity, how does the organization assess the potential? What about progress, performance and/or project outcomes? How does the organization respond when efforts produce less than favorable results or unintended consequences? How does it communicate about progress towards goals? How do acknowledge contributions?

high   low   high

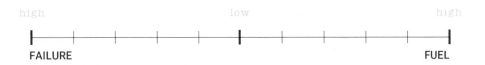

FAILURE   FUEL

ASSESSMENT

Reflection

○ What do you notice about your assessments?

○ Which force is exerting the most impact?

○ Where do you see the most (or least) balance? Is there integrity?

○ Are there strong similarities or differences across the three scales?

○ How might you use this scale to understand other stakeholders (i.e. team member, client, leader, etc.)?

NO.

04

PACE OF CHANGE

When to Change?

The rate of speed at which elements of a system can undergo change and adaptation given the information that is available at the time.

The term "analysis paralysis" describes the danger of being so inundated with possibilities and information and data that no action occurs; no decisions get made. Fear sets in and we freeze. In Business-As-Usual, this can happen at a large scale with big decisions and, more frequently, it shows up in our everyday interactions when someone suggests an idea and someone else responds with "that's not how we do it" or "we tried that before and it didn't work." This kind of assessment keeps us frozen in place, unable to move forward or try new things because we don't know which way to proceed.

In a Creativity Sustaining Atmosphere, speed is not the enemy; in fact it can be a great ally. It is possible to learn and adjust quickly when there is action. Rapid prototyping and deliberate experimentation help determine if a project or team is on the right path or it's time to pivot in another direction. We have to be willing to fail and the faster we fail, the better, because we learn more quickly and get closer to getting it right. This iterative approach fosters creative responsiveness in constantly changing environments because it provides constant feedback as projects progress.

"

It is only through
failure and through
experiment that
we learn and grow.

Isaac Stern

"

Frozen

An analysis-oriented approach to identifying opportunities and making decisions that is static and systematic.

....

When faced with a threat, our animal instincts consider a few primal options: fight (face the attack with aggression) or flight (remove oneself from the situation completely) or freeze (do nothing). Facing change involves facing a threat to what feels comfortable, it requires us to modify our behavior and do things differently than we normally do. So it's not surprising that some of our responses to change within organizations include Freeze, i.e. do nothing and hope the status quo endures, or move Fast, i.e. fight or

flight, doing something quickly to alter the current state.

The forces at play when it comes to innovation are similar- there are those people and organizations who prefer to avoid change and remain in a state of stasis, maintaining an equilibrium between the past, the present and the future. In this Frozen state, we hope that what has worked well in the past will continue to serve us and we resist making any sudden moves that threaten our feelings of comfort and

An action-oriented approach to identifying opportunities and making decisions quickly that is rapid and iterative.

. . . .

confidence. On the other hand, we have a strong force that pulls in the direction of accelerated change that is responsive and even, in some cases, reactionary.

Change is inevitable, how we respond to change is a choice. We can choose to stay still; to dig in our heels and hope that the same old ways of doing things will continue to work within new situations and a rapidly changing landscape. We can also choose to try something new, to respond in a different and unusual way that allows us to test out the potential of an alternative approach and assess the impact of our efforts. In a rapidly changing world, it is important that we can quickly identify opportunities and accelerate decision making or we risk getting left behind.

A beverage company was looking to redesign the package for its single-serve soft drinks. In fact, they had been trying to update the bottle design for nearly 10 years but had never come up with a design that tested better with consumers than what they already had.

So they never made a change. They were frozen.

The typical approach involved asking a creative agency to produce some sketches of different bottle designs, which were then tested with consumers in focus groups. They came to us for a new approach and a compressed timeline on the project, 6 months to design and engineer a consumer-preferred package and complete all of the necessary testing with manufacturing, filling, etc. They made it clear from the outset that a design would only be approved if we could demonstrate that it performed better than the current bottle with statistically significant results.

We proposed to move fast in a way that improved the likelihood of success by integrating consumer input throughout the short project cycle and aligning a core team of cross-functional experts from both our team and the client company. We started with generative research to inspire the design team and better understand the consumer needs. We conducted cocreation workshops with consumers and other key stakeholders. We also did immersive in-context interviewing that took us to people's home, cars, stores and behind the scenes of their beverage consuming habits and preferences.

The designers used insights from this work to generate sketches of six possible bottle designs and then worked with engineers to fine tune the concepts and produce prototypes that we were able to test with consumers in a second round of research. Because our participants were able to see the designs and feel them they provided valuable feedback for the development of the top three choices.

The cross-functional team of designers, engineers, and manufacturing experts then created authentic bottle prototypes of the final three designs that they could use to run tests for production, filling, etc. These final samples- filled, capped and labeled- showed exactly how the bottles would look and feel and function. We used them to conduct in-person research with 600 consumers who could touch them, open them up, drink soda from them and compare them to the current bottle design.

We were able to show, with a high degree of confidence, that 2 of the 3 concepts were preferred over the existing design. Thanks to parallel efforts to assess production and filling performance, we were ready to go into production once we had final results from the last round of consumer research. And the entire process took less than 6 months from start to finish.

In the same amount of time typically taken in the Business-As-Usual approach to generate some concept sketches and test them with consumers, we were able to produce two viable consumer-preferred designs. By iteratively increasing the fidelity of the prototypes to match the fidelity of the ideas, we were able to run three separate consumer research studies and conclude with manufacture-ready designs.

To foster a Creativity Sustaining Atmosphere for a project with such a brisk pace required involvement from a cross-functional team to ensure alignment and accelerate decision making. In addition to the successful project outcomes, our clients shared that the way we engaged their people was unlike anything that they had done in the past. It helped them to see that expert collaboration and alignment throughout the process made it possible to meet and exceed ambitious innovation goals.

What does it look
and feel like when an
organization, team or
individual is heavily
influenced by one
opposing force?

Frozen or Fast

FROZEN   FAST

Too Much Frozen

An organization that is Frozen refuses to consider new or alternative approaches that have not been tested or proven superior to familiar ways of doing things. Even if the face of competitive threats, the organization will stick with what has worked in the past and hope that it continues to work in the future. Oftentimes they have been around for a while and cling tightly to historically success ways of working. Even when strategic planning for the future, they are likely to avoid making any significant changes unless forced to do so by the market, regulations or consumer demand. In other words, when faced with opportunities, Frozen companies will react only when required to do so.

A Frozen Team is like a well-oiled machine that follows consistent processes and generates reliable outcomes. Their efforts are well-documented, successful and repeatable. These groups work best when doing the same work, the same way, every time. They appreciate standard operating procedures, templates, systems, and clear steps for project management. Frozen teams embrace data and metrics and may be slow to implement change when there is not enough compelling evidence to convince them. They are great at implementing. They are not so strong when it comes to identifying opportunities, imagining possibilities or generating lots of ideas. They tend to move cautiously and slowly when executing new approaches.

An Individual who exhibits too much Frozen favors routine, is skeptical of change and unwilling to try new things without a compelling reason to do so. They resist change (especially for the sake of change) and tend to only see opportunities that fit within existing, trusted systems. Likely a fan of data, facts and history, s/he especially appreciates stories that bring clear logic and reason to complex events and explain how decisions were made in the face of uncertainty and complexity. Frozen folks love organization, tidiness and systematizing things so that they are consistent, reliable and routine. They employ rationale, evidence-based decision making processes.

FROZEN   FAST

Too Much Fast

A Fast organization is overly responsive to external forces and willing to pivot quickly when faced with new opportunities. Sometimes it is fast first, rushing into unexplored terrain, or it can be a fast follower, quickly jumping on the successful bandwagon of competitors. This can result in brand confusion and an identity crisis as both customers and employees attempt to understand the mission and purpose of a constantly-changing company core. The too Fast company is incredibly agile and willing to try almost anything at least once which may stretch its resources and reputation to the point of deformation, so much so that the original identity is unrecognizable.

A team that moves too Fast goes quickly from task to task without pausing to assess or reflect the impact of their efforts. A collective love of action and motion prevents this team from staying still for long and they tend to make changes on the fly. It is easy for Fast teams to identify opportunities (and pursue them) because they are always on the lookout for things to change and improve. Sadly, moving so fast means that they may make decisions without deep consideration and/or documentation. Hence, these groups struggle to convince others of the value of their efforts or the merits of their processes (which are in flux and continuously changing). Fast teams may struggle to complete activities that are clearly defined and sequenced and the often make the same mistakes repeatedly because they don't take the time to learn from them.

When an individual is Fast, they are constantly on the move physically, mentally and figuratively. This person embraces novelty and loves trying new things simply because they are new and unfamiliar. Motivated by a deep sense of curiosity and adventure, the Fast individual will frequently dive into multiple exciting initiatives and may not stay around long enough to see any of them through to completion. Although willing to explore new processes and systems, this person is quickly bored by routine and has an aversion to doing the same thing in the same way over and over again.

Assessment Using the Scales

Use the scale to assess the tension between these two opposing forces of Frozen and Fast. Place a mark on each side of the scale, one for each force. The closer the mark is to either end of the spectrum, the stronger the pull. The closer to the center the mark is, the less force is exerted by that side.

This is not an "either/or" choice, rather you will indicate the strength of each force on both sides and then connect these marks to create a bar that illustrates the tension between the two. The wider the bar, the stronger the tension (both forces exerting strong influence), while a shorter bar represents less tension (neither force exerting strong influence). The goal is balance and, ideally, a wider bar. A shorter bar often indicates that there is not enough of either force to produce the kind of creative tension necessary for truly breakthrough innovation.

Consider how you, your team and your organization set the pace of change. What is the comfortable cruising speed? For each of the following scales representing elements of the system, indicate the strength of the pull of Frozen by placing a mark on the left side. Indicate the strength of the pull of Fast by placing a mark on the right side. Once you have marks on either side, connect them to create a bar that demonstrates the width and location along the scale.

You. Consider yourself first. When faced with a challenge or opportunity, do you slow down or speed up? Do you prefer to gather information or jump in and figure it out as you go? Are you more skeptical or curious about change?

high   low   high

FROZEN   FAST

Your team. Pick a team that you work with and consider how, in general the team sets a pace of change. When faced with a challenge or opportunity, do you slow down or speed up? Do you prefer to gather information or jump in and figure it out as you go? Are you more skeptical or curious about change? Are your processes developed and systematic or more emergent and on-the-fly? How do you make decisions together? How do you reference past efforts?

high   low   high

FROZEN   FAST

Your organization. Now think about your organization as a whole. When faced with a challenge or opportunity, does the organization slow down or speed up? Does it prefer to gather information or jump in and figure it out? Is it more skeptical or curious about change? Are organizational processes developed and systematic or more emergent and on-the-fly? What are the norms for decision making? How does the organization (formally and informally) regard its history and future?

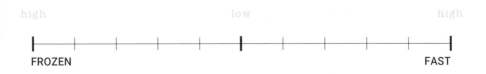

high   low   high

FROZEN   FAST

○ What do you notice about your assessments?

○ Which force is exerting the most impact?

○ Where do you see the most (or least) balance? Is there integrity?

○ Are there strong similarities or differences across the three scales?

○ How might you use this scale to understand other stakeholders (i.e. team member, client, leader, etc.)?

NO.

05

AMBIGUITY

How to Adapt?
Tolerance for uncertainty and willingness to proceed
with a plan that is likely to change during the course of
implementation.

Most organizations are successful precisely because they embrace the
familiar; familiar ways of doing things that foster a sense of comfort,
confidence and consistency for employees, customers, investors, etc.
We can take Familiarity for granted because it is all around us in what we
see and say and do and think. In Business-As-Usual, familiar processes
and protocols that have been the key to success in the past are rarely
questioned. They may be wielded as weapons to squash suggestions
that deviate from the norm. Unfortunately, incredible opportunities can be
rejected when considered within the context of how well they fit into the tried
and true approach because that's just not "how we do things around here".

Familiarity may actually prevent future success if it blinds us to new
possibilities, which is why it is necessary to consider those things that
feel uncomfortable and Foreign. Strange and unusual stimuli are catalysts
for creativity that spark new ways of thinking and alternative solutions to
problems. In a Creativity Sustaining Atmosphere, it is important to look
beyond what we know and what we believe and make space to explore
alternative points of view and experiences. When we get too comfortable
with what's familiar, we risk missing opportunities and responding to
change. When we refuse to acknowledge and embrace that which we
don't understand, we lose the potential for generating new thinking and
breakthroughs that transform our industries and ourselves.

66

Discovery consists
in seeing what
everyone else has
seen and thinking
what no one else
has thought.

Albert von
Szent-Gyorgyi

99

Familiar

Dependence upon known, comfortable and (oftentimes) traditional approaches to identifying opportunities and making decisions.

. . . .

Albert Einstein cleverly pointed out that doing the same thing over and over while expecting different results is, essentially, insanity. If you seek the same dependable outcomes and the situation remains fairly stable, it's a fine strategy to keep doing things the way we've always done them. It can be valuable to keep talking to the same people, utilizing the same processes, and consistently generating the same products. The challenge arises when we desire new outcomes, when what we get for our efforts isn't exactly what we (or others) want.

We often taken for granted what feels Familiar. We barely recognize our own habits and patterns of thinking and doing because they no longer require our deliberate thought and attention. That's because the brain is a self-optimizing muscle. It strengthens the neural connections that we use most frequently, coating well-travelled pathways with myelin to increase the speed of transmission. Driving to work is a classic example – we have taken the same route so many times that our brain no longer has to allocate processing power to the activity. We are on auto-pilot.

Foreign

Willingness to utilize unknown, unfamiliar and (oftentimes) uncomfortable approaches to identifying opportunities and making decisions.

....

This functionality demonstrates the connection between repetitive actions and improved performance. It also reveals a cognitive bias towards the familiar and an often-unconscious tendency to take the road most traveled. So what happens when there is no existing road that will take us where we want to go? We have to take a cognitive detour; to venture into unfamiliar territories of thinking and doing.

If we are willing to get off the beaten path of tradition we can explore ways that feel Foreign. As we build the capacity to navigate diverse landscapes we learn to leverage ambiguity as a means for discovering new ways of solving the same old (yet always changing) problems. An alternative route to work will always feel Foreign until the first time that we take it.

Executives at a global mining company were planning a weeklong retreat with the leadership team for a business unit that had recently undergone reorganization. Such efforts often throw employees into a state of ambiguity where familiar processes and people are unsettled and foreign ways of doing things become the norm. They hoped that gathering the team members from around the world to spend time together would promote collaboration and foster alignment around a common strategic vision. The agenda was filled with standard Business-As-Usual fare: long days of presentations and discussions (and then more presentations).

Most of the attendees were in unfamiliar territory geographically and linguistically. The session took place in the U.S. and they came from around the world. English was not necessarily the primary language for everyone. Additionally, this marked the first occasion for the entire group to be in the same location together.

They represented vast diversity in terms of their areas of expertise (i.e. business and operational, technical and scientific). They each brought different levels of experience with the industry and the organization. They had diverse cultural norms. Each had a distinct point of view about the future of their business. The one thing that they all had in common was a desire to collaborate on a strategic vision and find a path forward together.

Fortunately, one enlightened leader was also on a mission to inspire creative thinking in the attendees through the use of an unusual approach: play. We agreed to facilitate one-day of the retreat using Lego® Serious Play® (LSP) methods and materials. LSP requires people to build models of ideas and challenges using the colorful interlocking bricks.

Our session was on the fourth day of the retreat and intended to provide an opportunity for engaging discussions about the week's presentations. It was also meant to foster hands-on interaction among attendees in a Creativity Sustaining Atmosphere. We certainly faced a lot of skeptical scowls and raised eyebrows from tired attendees,

We also saw eagerness for a fresh change of pace and a new approach to strategic visioning.

Our playfully productive approach was pretty foreign to nearly everyone in the room (a few had experienced LSP before). Fortunately, participants used the technique to help them communicate things that they are very familiar with: their perspective on their work, challenges they face and help solve, and their own hopes for bringing value to their company and stakeholders. These constructive conversations ensured every single person in the room had a voice and that they could actually see what the others were saying and build upon it. Working individually and collaboratively, the group eventually emerged with a clear understanding of their internal resources and opportunities plus a strong vision for the next three years and how they would collaborate to reach their goals.

The unusual process provided a chance for people to relax, laugh, explore, have meaningful conversations and get to know each other better. There was considerably more alignment around a vision for the future than anyone expected and everyone agreed that the approach made it easy to interact and arrive at common goals and initiatives. The biggest (self-proclaimed) skeptic in the room was the Chief Financial Officer. In the end he admitted that he was astonished by how much valuable hard work was accomplished with a technique that felt like child's play. He added that he would be happy to approve funding for additional sessions and efforts that utilized this foreign (now familiar) approach.

What does it look and feel like when an organization, team or individual is heavily influenced by one *opposing force?*

Familiar or Foreign

FAMILIAR   FOREIGN

Too Much Familiar

An organization that is dominated by the Familiar is quite comfortable with the ways things have always been done largely due to success with traditional ways of doing things. It is likely perceived as a reliable and steady entity by internal and external stakeholders (i.e. customers and employees). Operations run smoothly, like a well-oiled machine, and have been refined and continuously improved over the years. There are strong cultural norms to abide by (i.e. "how we do things around here") and significant skepticism about any deviation from standardized procedures. These organizations often have a substantial percentage of employees with long-term tenure and may ignore signs that change is impending.

Teams that are overly Familiar tend to succeed well using a systematic approach that has withstood the test of time. Noted for their strong performance and ability to meet goals, they are incredibly reliable when things proceed according to well-thought out plans and struggle when they don't. These teams are well-suited for precision tasks that require repeatability and consistency. They are not prepared to respond quickly to unexpected outcomes or unintended consequences of their efforts.

A Familiar-focused Individual is quite comfortable and set in their ways. They prefer to use reliable, trusted techniques and resources to identify opportunities and make logical decisions. With deep expertise and a historical understanding of how things have worked best in the past, they may be skeptical of new people and processes. They tend to resist the adoption of new information, techniques or team members. Reliable systems and repeatability are of the utmost importance for the individual who embraces the Familiar. They enjoy routines and avoid last minute activities that disrupt their sense of order.

FAMILIAR   FOREIGN

Too Much Foreign

When an organization is under too much influence of the Foreign, it is adaptable and flexible enough to rapidly respond to change from outside forces. The willingness to embrace the unusual has probably earned it the reputation of being innovative and responsive to market, industry and culture trends. This organizational agility may produce uncertainty in the market and internally if change happens too quickly and stakeholders perceive a lack of reliability and structure. Absence of institutional memory and appreciation for past efforts may lead to disillusioned or frustrated employees and weaken brand loyalty.

A team that is heavily dominated by a desire to pursue the Foreign is fearless about leaping into unfamiliar territory and exploring new opportunities. They are likely avid consumers of trends and prefer to try new approaches and technology rather than use something familiar that has already been proven effective. They may be considered cutting edge and cavalier in their efforts to stay ahead of uncertainty by taking risks and frequently leaping into the unknown. Teams that love the Foreign are considered go-to sources for innovative thinking, especially when faced with a particularly wicked problem for which there is no precedent. They likely have many fans and critics.

An individual who embraces the Foreign may be a pleasure-seeker who is constantly on the lookout for interesting new stimulus and information. Quick to say "yes" to an invitation or opportunity to experience something for the first time, they may appear to have a short attention span or seem unreliable given their tendency to be easily distracted. They resist repetition and, when faced with a familiar activity, enjoy creating alternative ways to do the same old thing. The individual who thrives on the Foreign may shift around a lot (among teams or departments) because once a situation starts to feel too familiar to them the thrill is gone and it's time to move on.

AMBIGUITY

Assessment Using the Scales

Use the scale to assess the tension between these two opposing forces of Familiar and Foreign. Place a mark on each side of the scale, one for each force. The closer the mark is to either end of the spectrum, the stronger the pull. The closer to the center the mark is, the less force is exerted by that side.

This is not an "either/or" choice, rather you will indicate the strength of each force on both sides and then connect these marks to create a bar that illustrates the tension between the two. The wider the bar, the stronger the tension (both forces exerting strong influence), while a shorter bar represents less tension (neither force exerting strong influence). The goal is balance and, ideally, a wider bar. A shorter bar often indicates that there is not enough of either force to produce the kind of creative tension necessary for truly breakthrough innovation.

Consider how you, your team and your organization face ambiguity. When faced with uncertainty, how do you respond? For each of the following scales representing elements of the system, indicate the strength of the pull of Familiar by placing a mark on the left side. Indicate the strength of the pull of Foreign by placing a mark on the right side. Once you have marks on either side, connect them to create a bar that demonstrates the width and location along the scale.

You. Consider yourself first. When you face uncertainty, how do you respond? Do you prefer to look inwards and backwards and, i.e. at what you are comfortable with because it has worked before in the past? Or do you prefer to look forward, i.e. into unfamiliar spaces and face the unknown in hopes that you might finds clues for new insights or approaches? When ambiguity arises, do you seek to stabilize or revolutionize?

high   low   high

FAMILIAR   **FOREIGN**

Your team. Pick a team that you work with and consider how, in general the team responds to uncertainty. Do you prefer to look inwards and backwards and, i.e. at what you are comfortable with because it has worked before in the past? Or do you prefer to look forward, i.e. into unfamiliar spaces and face the unknown in hopes that you might finds clues for new insights or approaches? When ambiguity arises, do you seek to stabilize or revolutionize? How do you make these decisions together and navigate the ambiguity?

high   low   high

FAMILIAR   **FOREIGN**

Your organization. Now think about your organization as a whole and how it responds to uncertainty. Does it prefer to look inwards and backwards and, i.e. at what is comfortable and familiar because it has worked in the past? Or does it foster a forward-looking approach and encourage people to look into unfamiliar spaces and face the unknown to find clues for new insights or approaches? Does the organization actively pursue new opportunities through study of unfamiliar markets, business models, etc.? When ambiguity arises, does the organization seek to stabilize or revolutionize?

high   low   high

FAMILIAR   **FOREIGN**

Reflection

○ What do you notice about your assessments?

○ Which force is exerting the most impact?

○ Where do you see the most (or least) balance? Is there integrity?

○ Are there strong similarities or differences across the three scales?

○ How might you use this scale to understand other stakeholders (i.e. team member, client, leader, etc.)?

NO.

06

PLAYING FIELD

Who Matters?

Understanding key stakeholders who impact and are impacted, awareness of context and landscape that shapes decision making.

Today's Business-As-Usual environments are fiercely competitive, characterized by a drive to gain a winning advantage over those who seek the same outcome. We see this in how companies compete for customers and brand awareness. We also see it internally, within organizations, in how employees compete with each other for projects, positions and credit. The competitive drive can fuel growth and spur a healthy growth trajectory. It can also inspire hard work and discretionary effort in pursuit of goals.

There is certainly nothing inherently wrong with "competition" per se, however it may set up a paradigm of winning and losing, of "us versus them", that can be detrimental to innovation efforts. In a competitive environment, the goal of winning can overshadow opportunities to learn from those we seek to defeat and blind us to potential for collaboration or some friendly "co-opetition" among those who seek the same stakeholder benefits. A Creativity Sustaining Atmosphere is one that recognizes the value of each "player" on the field and actively seeks to identify ways to benefit as many stakeholders as possible. One saying goes "the high tide raises all ships" and so it is when we act as friends and attempt to bring forward the best possible outcome for all concerned.

" Goodwill is the
only asset that
competition
cannot undersell
or destroy.

Marshall Field **"**

Fierce

Relying primarily upon the competitive landscape and a drive to remove potential threats during opportunity identification and decision making.

. . . .

Oftentimes when hoping to evolve or innovate, we look around us to see what others are doing. We survey individuals or organizations that do what we do to see what is working for them and how we might do it better. We look at the competitive landscape to identify opportunities so we are prepared to make decisions about where to invest or obtain resources, approval, etc. Basically, we play to win. And when we play to win, we inevitably create a situation where someone else (or many others) will lose.

Today's business and organizational landscapes are complicated and volatile. It is not unusual that we feel the need to fiercely pursue our goals and protect ourselves from competition. This can lead to a narrow view of the playing field.

When we become so focused on the game that we are playing, the other players and the rules then we lose sight of other possibilities. We get so busy being on the offensive or defensive that we stop seeing the bigger picture. We lose sight of the potential for an experience or outcome that is beneficial for everyone.

Recent breakthroughs in products and services demonstrate the potential for significant disruption when we are willing to radically rethink the playing field, the players

Friends

Considering divergent points of view and the potential for mutually beneficial outcomes when identifying opportunities and making decisions.

and, even, the rules of the game. As we explore the strengths of our competitors and even treat them like friends, as we look for new players to join the game, we begin to open up new ways of thinking about solving problems.

Take, for example, companies like Netflix, Uber and AirBnb. These game changers recognized the great potential of leveraging relationships with a whole new set of players that previously weren't even invited to play. Netflix changed the video rental playing field to our mailboxes and streaming sources. Uber recruited a whole new team of players, regular people who may never have been taxi drivers or customers but were quite willing to provide a new kind of service. AirBnB changed the field and the players by creating a game where anyone can host a guest in their home and we can explore the world in a new way.

For each of these companies, breakthrough success required them to think differently about the playing field. They identified ways to create and leverage relationships (between video rental and mail delivery, between car owners and riders, between home owners and travelers). By acting as friends and generating opportunities to connect people, it is possible to transform a win/lose paradigm into a situation that generates a win for everyone involved.

A national quick serve restaurant chain was preparing to develop new menu platforms for the following year. These platforms, offered for a limited time, include items above and beyond the standard menu fare and typically coincide with seasonal or cultural events.

Feeling increasing pressure from other national chains, they planned to convene a large group of key stakeholders for a multi-day offsite session to explore ideas and align around new menu offerings. For this group, Business-As-Usual involved benchmarking their biggest competitors and identifying opportunities for a competitive advantage with their target market.

As we prepared for the session, we realized that a lot of the competition for customers' mealtime actually came from local "mom and pop" restaurants. We also discovered in social media reviews that the negative feedback typically came from diners who favored smaller restaurants and gave more favorable rankings to their local favorites. The client was initially skeptical of the value of focusing on the needs of customers who didn't frequent the larger chains and who not likely to become part of their core target market.

We suggested a different approach to fostering a Creativity Sustaining Atmosphere in the session by "befriending" the enemy. We created cross-functional forager teams made up of key internal stakeholders (i.e. marketing, chefs, etc.) plus external partners (i.e. creative agency, franchise owners, etc.), i.e. the usual suspects. Each team also included a local diner; someone who favored locally owned restaurants and tended to criticize the larger chains, i.e. a resident expert.

We sent the teams out into the wild, on "meal safaris", to dine at local favorites and explore what made them great, from a customer point of view.

Post-safari discussions revealed a ton of insight about how these smaller diners offered a competitive advantage in terms of the menu and the customer experience.

We encouraged the client to think small and get friendly with local diners rather than fiercely focusing on their national chain competitors. Through this experience of "dining with the enemy" and discussing the experience afterwards, teams were able to identify a number of insights about the

emotional connection that people bring to mealtime and the kinds of food that foster a sense of comfort and nostalgia.

These insights translated into a large quantity and diversity of compelling concepts that provided more than enough menu platforms for the following year. Teams felt connected and aligned around criteria for choosing which platforms to pursue. The experience also helped the client identify additional opportunities beyond the menu that could significantly improve the diner experience.

What does it look and feel like when an organization, team or individual is heavily influenced by one *opposing force?*

FIERCE   FRIENDS

Too Much Fierce

An organization that is dominated by a paradigm of Fierce competition is acutely aware of the diverse influences on its success, constantly tracking and reporting diverse metrics to diagnose and predict performance (both internally and externally). Motivated by a strong desire to beat out competitors, Fierce organizations prioritize exclusivity over inclusivity and strategic advantage over collective good. Externally these organizations may be perceived as ruthless, aggressive and of questionable ethics which is reflected by an internal culture of strong hierarchy and privilege of status. Organizational ferocity is also evidenced by rigid control of access to people and opportunities.

When a team is particularly Fierce, it can be very successful within a Fierce organization as it is likely to have mastered the "rules of the game" and moves nimbly in response to various threats to its performance. A cohesive team of interdependent players who collaborate well and rely on each other may be incredibly successful on the outside yet, internally, suffer from infighting or other behaviors that reflect an inherent distrust and fear that other members will put their own needs above the needs of the team.

A Fierce individual is likely adept at navigating the organizational playing field and quick to ascend the ranks or acquire coveted positions and status. This one knows how to distinguish themselves from others in the pack and communicate their unique value to the organization or team. Possibly a lone ranger in the organization who strategically pursues his/her own agenda; the Fierce employee is successful but may be disliked or distrusted by others. The Fierce are quick to identify opportunities and make decision that advance personal goals.

FIERCE   FRIENDS

Too Much Friends

A Friendly organization is inclusive and equally responsive to the needs and potential of all of its stakeholders, including competitors. While a Friendly organization is often perceived well by customers and employees, it can also succumb to its own benevolence and fail to make tough decisions that benefit the business but leave some people unhappy. For example, a friendly organization may have very happy and engaged employees who don't perform well and are not held accountable or it may continue longstanding vendor relationships with strong personal connections that are no longer financially beneficial. When competition is not a strong driving force, the organization may become myopically focused on internal influences and lag behind competitors or miss out on opportunities.

An overly Friendly team gets along very well, maybe too well, and is marked by an ability to operate in ways that are beneficial to everyone and leverage team member strengths while compensating for any deficits. Unfortunately, when team members are too Friendly and are overly sensitive to each other's needs they may avoid challenging or questioning each other for fear of damaging relationships. There may be difficulties with focus or convergence because every idea seems like a good one and every voice carries equal weight. Friendly teams may inadvertently become insular if they overprioritize their own needs, eventually isolating themselves from others within the organization.

When an individual is too Friendly, s/he becomes a trusted source and advisor for peers and is described as a good listener, thoughtful communicator and diplomatic decision maker. Willing to consider the needs of many, the Friend will often identify solutions that promote harmony and satisfy the seemingly divergent goals of many stakeholders. For the overly Friendly is can be a struggle to set clear boundaries with others and difficult to initiate critical conversations that may upset others or hurt someone's feelings and compromise an interpersonal relationship. Friendly individuals may struggle to assert themselves and their needs or avoid competitive situations where there is a clear winner and loser.

Assessment Using the Scales

Use the scale to assess the tension between these two opposing forces of Fierce and Friends. Place a mark on each side of the scale, one for each force. The closer the mark is to either end of the spectrum, the stronger the pull. The closer to the center the mark is, the less force is exerted by that side.

This is not an "either/or" choice, rather you will indicate the strength of each force on both sides and then connect these marks to create a bar that illustrates the tension between the two. The wider the bar, the stronger the tension (both forces exerting strong influence), while a shorter bar represents less tension (neither force exerting strong influence). The goal is balance and, ideally, a wider bar. A shorter bar often indicates that there is not enough of either force to produce the kind of creative tension necessary for truly breakthrough innovation.

Consider how you, your team and your organization see the playing field. What kind of game is it? Are you playing to win at all costs? For each of the following scales representing elements of the system, indicate the strength of the pull of Fierce by placing a mark on the left side. Indicate the strength of the pull of Friends by placing a mark on the right side. Once you have marks on either side, connect them to create a bar that demonstrates the width and location along the scale.

You. Consider yourself first. When you consider the landscape of your work environment, how do you feel about your role and position? Are you a team member or a competitor? Do you prefer to distinguish yourself or align with others? How do consider others when you make decisions? When faced with a challenge or opportunity, do you slow down or speed up? Do you prefer to gather information or jump in and figure it out as you go? Are you more skeptical or curious about change?

high   low   high

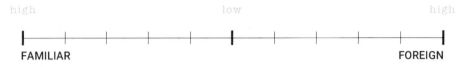

FAMILIAR   FOREIGN

 Your team. Pick a team that you work with and consider how, in general, the team considers the landscape of the work environment. How do you feel about your role and position? Are you part of a greater team or competing with others for resources and status? Do you prefer to distinguish your team's efforts or align with others? How do consider other teams and individuals when making decisions?

high   low   high

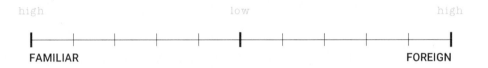

FAMILIAR   FOREIGN

 Your organization. Now think about your organization as a whole. How does the organization consider the work and competitive landscape? How does it feel about role and position? Is it part of a greater entity (industry, market, society) or competing with others for resources and status? Does the organization prefer to distinguish itself or align with others? How does it consider other entities and competition when making decisions?

high   low   high

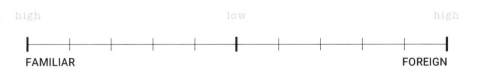

FAMILIAR   FOREIGN

Reflection

○ What do you notice about your assessments?

○ Which force is exerting the most impact?

○ Where do you see the most (or least) balance? Is there integrity?

○ Are there strong similarities or differences across the three scales?

○ How might you use this scale to understand other stakeholders (i.e. team member, client, leader, etc.)?

This section described the six dimensions where challenges arise and make innovation difficult because of opposing forces that create tension during transformation efforts.

Knowledge
BAU   CSA
FACTS   FEELINGS

Risk
BAU   CSA
FEAR   FAITH

Assessment
BAU   CSA
FAILURE   FUEL

Pace of Change
BAU   CSA
FROZEN   FAST

Ambiguity
BAU   CSA
FAMILIAR   FOREIGN

Playing Field
BAU   CSA
FIERCE   FRIENDS

So what makes innovation so hard? It all comes down to people and place. People (including ourselves) bring essential expertise to the task at hand. They (we) also bring personal beliefs, preferences and biases for one force opposed to the other. Our place of work, i.e. our organization as well as the many groups and teams with which we affiliate and collaborate, also shape our innovation efforts by asserting pressure upon us according to their own biases towards different forces.

If we want to do something about all of this, we have to recognize the people and places that influence our work and navigate these challenges by modulating our own behaviors. As Ghandi put it, we must be the change we want to see. As innovators, we must model the very mindset that we hope to cultivate in others.

This means we must empathize with diverse needs for knowledge, have courage to face risk, embrace our potential for evolution when faced with assessment, experiment with different paces of change, be curious about what we can't predict or know, and be willing to connect with others who have impact or are impacted by our actions.

In the next section we turn our attention to the processes and projects where the hard work of innovation actually happens. Let's explore what to do about these tensions and how to navigate the journey of transforming an existing situation to a preferred one.

WHAT TO
DO ABOUT IT

In the first section of this book, we focused on the six different dimensions of tension that make innovation efforts so F-ing hard. So now we understand why innovation feels difficult but don't worry! Innovation doesn't have to hurt. The key to navigating innovation challenges is Facilitation. The root of the word facilitation is FACIL which comes from Greek and means easy. In essence, **to facilitate is to make it easy for others to do something.**

F-ing innovation is the practice of facilitating innovation in a way that eases the tensions of transformation.

In this section we are going to roll up our sleeves and explore how to remedy imbalances and ease the tensions of transformation using the innovation facilitator's mindset. For each dimension there is a corresponding attitude or behavior that provides a remedy for imbalance. Together, these six attitudes comprise the innovation facilitator's mindset, a way of thinking and doing and being during transformation design in pursuit of new, innovative ways of working.

Each tension can be understood in terms of both impact (the strength of each force resulting in the distance of the tension) and integrity (the equilibrium between the two forces, resulting in the balance of the tension). How to apply the suggested remedy will depend upon the diagnosis and the people involved.

Remember, the goal is not to remove or eliminate the tension. The tension itself is beneficial and helps produce creative breakthroughs. When there is low impact (i.e. minimal tension) the goal is actually to increase the tension. When there is low integrity (i.e. imbalanced tensions) then the goal is to balance the tension by exerting influence in the other direction. Ideally there will be a strong tension that is balanced and a strong facilitator who can bring out the best of both when everyone meets in the middle.

Knowledge
empathy
▼

BAU   CSA

FACTS   FEELINGS

Risk
courage
▼

BAU   CSA

FEAR   FAITH

Assessment
evolution
▼

BAU   CSA

FAILURE   FUEL

Pace of Change
experimentation
▼

BAU   CSA

FROZEN   FAST

Ambiguity
curiosity
▼

BAU   CSA

FAMILIAR   FOREIGN

Playing Field
connection
▼

BAU   CSA

FIERCE   FRIENDS

Every situation is unique because of the people, the context, the history and more. This means there is no one perfect remedy for the ways that you are experiencing tension. A key task of any innovator is to understand how to diagnose the source of tension and adjust behavior accordingly (i.e. increase curiosity or decrease empathy).

The following section describes how to leverage the innovation facilitator's mindset to ease the tensions of transformation. For each tension you will find many questions that serve as points of departure to explore solutions. Your task is to design and apply a remedy that is appropriate for your situation. As you practice these skills and learn from your experiences you will be on a path towards mastery as an innovation facilitator.

THE SOURCE OF TENSION IS: KNOWLEDGE

Knowledge is related to what constitutes knowledge used for decision making, including how information is generated, communicated and prioritized in order to make it actionable.

It responds to the question "How to know?"

Tension related to knowledge is created by the opposing forces of Facts and Feelings. Facts are not better than Feelings. Feelings are not better than Facts. They are both valuable when pursuing innovative solutions. They can also be difficult to balance so it is helpful to diagnose which Force may be exerting too much influence on a process, project or individual and remedy that imbalance with **Empathy.**

▶ Empathy is the ability to understand the experience of another, to walk in someone else's shoes and see the world as they do.

Empathy is a learnable skill, though it does take practice. The most important element of Empathy is intention- the fundamental desire to explore a situation from someone else's point of view with a genuine willingness to have your own perceptions transformed.

To practice empathy, you must first identify who or what you want to better understand. Then develop an approach for engaging different people in meaningful discussions about their experience. Practice active listening and be willing to have your thinking provoked or transformed by what you learn.

FACTS   FEELINGS

Knowledge provides inspiration and information that fuels opportunity identification and decision making. When the span of knowledge is small it means that knowledge seeking is not a strong priority. If no one is asking "What do we know?" or "How do we know that?" then no one is attempting to answer those questions. To increase the impact of knowledge means to collect, curate and communicate relevant information.

Apply an Empathy mindset to increase the impact of knowledge.

Use Empathy to explore how knowledge can be useful for you, different groups or your organization as a whole. You may choose the role of provocateur, i.e. asking questions that force others to seek new knowledge. Maybe you prefer to assume the responsibility of researcher- finding and sharing information that is valuable. Or you might be the broadcaster who shares information others have collected, making sure it is available to a broad audience for widespread impact.

The questions below are starting points to help you think about the kind of knowledge that is relevant for your situation, team, organization, etc.

. . . .

What is known, not known, assumed?

What might these stakeholders want or need to learn more about?

Consider specific topics that are obviously important like rules and regulations, customer insights, industry trends, adjacent markets, etc. Think about what is not obvious and even what seems frivolous or ridiculous. Inspiration often comes from unusual or seemingly unrelated areas.

Who wants to know? Who needs to know?

Who are the different stakeholders that would benefit from more knowledge? Empathize with stakeholders inside of your organization like leaders, colleagues, peers, team members, other employees, other divisions or departments, etc.

Empathize with external stakeholders like customers, users, vendors, partners, competitors, investors, etc. Empathize with yourself and consider what you are curious about.

Where can we find what we want to know?

Where can answers to the questions be found?

Consider both primary (direct) and secondary (indirect) sources of information. Explore both internal and external resources. Look in usual locations; those that are familiar and reliable. Also think about unusual sources of information that provide an alternative perspective or even contrasting viewpoint.

How do they prefer to know?

What formats are available for packaging information in a way that is easy to understand?

Consider the different stakeholders involved and what kind of information they value (i.e. Facts or Feelings). Think about how to present information in a "language" that makes sense to the audience. It might be visual (like a diagram, presentation, video, etc.) or more verbal (using words, stories, or audio) or even interactive (i.e. fill in the blank, games, etc.).

When to know?

What is the appropriate time to share information?

Consider how it may be used to inspire or inform decisions. Identify the optimal timing for providing information so that is has the most value and impact.

Improve Integrity: How to Balance

Apply an Empathy mindset to increase the integrity of knowledge.
Empathy for key stakeholders helps balance the opposing forces of Facts
and Feelings. When these forces are in equilibrium it means that you are
getting the best of both worlds and leveraging diverse strengths. Balance
signifies integrity.

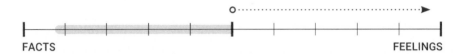

FACTS   FEELINGS

Striking the Balance: How to Remedy too much Facts

If there is too much influence from Facts, turn up the Empathy and explore
the Feelings of the humans involved. Seek information that complements
the Facts through to foster a deeper understanding of why they matter
and how they are experienced. This additional information can reveal new
opportunities, expose threats and improve confidence with decisions.

How might we apply Empathy to bring integrity to our Facts?
Some questions to ask that help diagnose where some Feelings could help:

Who is impacted by this and how do they feel about it?
You may need to consider internal stakeholders, like team members or other
employees, and external stakeholders like customers, users, partners or
competitors. Consider the data that you have and what stories you can find
that will foster a deeper understanding of what you know.

Who else should we be talking to?
There are likely many stakeholders involved in any challenge you are facing
so think about who else has an opinion or need that can shed some light on
your data.

Why is this important or not?
Are you confident that you have a clear understanding of why the facts
matter? Do you need to learn more?

What might change? Are we prepared to respond?
If the Facts are quantitative and numeric, balance them with more qualitative
and narrative types of information.

FACTS   FEELINGS

Striking the Balance: How to Remedy too much Feelings

If Feelings are taking over, turn down the Empathy and look to balance what you feel or intuitively believe with more Facts and objective information to inform decision making. When we use Facts and Feelings together we balance these forces to develop a richer understanding of the situation. This allows us to generate insights that yield product creative tension.

How might we apply Empathy to bring integrity to our Feelings?
Some questions to ask that help diagnose where some Facts could help:

What assumptions do we have?
Identify anything that may be taken for granted or be the result of bias. Consider how to balance intuition with data.

What issues cause emotions to run high? Why?
Look at topics or decisions that elicit intense response. Emotions are strong indicators of issues that may benefit from some objective information.

What do the critics say? Why?
Don't ignore the naysayers, they may have valid reasons for conflicting opinions. Consider alternative viewpoints and the rationale behind them.

How do our desires align with strategic goals?
It is easy to be swayed by exciting, shiny ideas. Keep potential distractions in check with logical consideration of the long-term vision.

EMPATHY

THE SOURCE OF TENSION IS: RISK

Risk is related to orientation to vulnerability and exposure to potential loss, including the degree of willingness to try something new without certainty of outcomes.

It responds to the question "What's at stake?"

Tension related to risk is created by the opposing forces of Fear and Faith. Faith is not better than Fear. Fear is not better than Faith. They are both valuable when pursuing innovative solutions. They can also be difficult to balance so it is valuable to diagnose which Force may be exerting too much influence on a process, project or individual and remedy that imbalance with a **Courage** mindset.

► Courage means having the heart to face that which we fear.

In order to innovate, we must be willing to fear less. Fear itself is not wrong or undesirable so long as it is not overwhelming. In fact, it can be quite helpful in mitigating risk and managing sustainable growth. However, we have to recognize that transformation involves letting go of the past (or at least parts of it) so that we can move forward.

Pablo Picasso said that "Every act of creation is first an act of destruction" and so it is with efforts to create a more innovation-friendly organization. We must be willing to destroy old ways of thinking that are irrelevant or outdated. Especially if they no longer serve us in an ever-changing and increasingly complex landscape. This makes room for us to experiment with creating something new.

Yes, this is scary, but when we adopt a "fear less" mindset we embrace our enthusiasm and channel that energy towards the desired outcomes. The more we are willing to face what we fear, the less restricted we are by what we don't know or understand, and the more powerful we become.

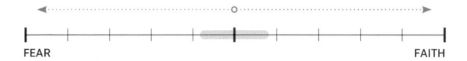

FEAR   FAITH

The saying goes, "no risk, no reward." Risk provides the potential for growth and improvement beyond the present situation. When the span of risk is small it means that there is little awareness of the stakes, including what might be gained and what might be lost.

Apply a Courage mindset to increase the impact of risk.

Use Courage to develop self-awareness as an organization, team or individual. Get vulnerable and take an honest look in the mirror to identify potential opportunities for growth and dangers. Increasing impact through risk means figuring out how to grow in way that balances risk with reward.

The questions below are starting points to help you think about the ways to strategically leverage risk in order to improve yourself, situation, team, organization, etc. Think of the acronym GROWTH to easily remember these questions.

. . . .

What are we Great at?

What are the internal strengths you are willing to protect and defend?

Consider capabilities and unique expertise. Think about the value you offer including the history or experience you have delivering it. Think about resources that make you distinct; that you can't afford to lose.

"What Risks do we face?"

What external factors, beyond your control, threaten your success?

Explore the factors that threaten your greatness. Risks can be environmental, cultural, digital, regulatory, political, interpersonal, etc. Include risks that others are willing to take that may change the competitive landscape.

What Opportunities are available to us?

What external events or activities might benefit from your greatness?

Identify new areas to apply your greatness and bring value. Look at your current context and explore new areas of opportunity that may be nearby/adjacent or radically different.

What are our Weaknesses?

What is happening internally that makes you feel vulnerable?

Consider internal threats to your resources and strengths. Identify things that may compromise capabilities, expertise, effectiveness, etc. including how they may be impacted by time and technology.

What Trends may have an impact?

Which movements could benefit or damage you?

Think about the opportunities and challenges that may emerge depending on changing needs, desires and values of consumers or other key stakeholders. Inspire yourself by considering how trends related to diverse industries and contexts may relate to you.

Who can Help us?

Who are your current or potential partners?

You don't have to go it alone. Recognize the potential collaborators you already have in your midst. Discover new possibilities that might benefit from your strengths or defend your weak spots.

Improve Integrity: How to Balance

Apply a Courage mindset to increase the integrity of risk.
Courage to be vulnerable and try new things helps balance the opposing
forces of Fear and Faith. When these forces are in equilibrium it means that
you are getting the best of both worlds and leveraging diverse strengths.
Balance signifies integrity.

FEAR   FAITH

Striking the Balance: How to Remedy too much Fear

If there is too much influence from Fear, dial up the Courage and bring
awareness to the source of discomfort. Facing fear begins with identifying
vulnerabilities and understanding how they impede risk. Look your fears in
the eye and walk towards them.

How might we apply Courage to bring integrity to our Fear?
Some questions to ask that help diagnose where some Faith could help:

What are we afraid to talk about?
Fears are found in the hushed conversations that happen behind closed
doors or get prefaced with "You didn't hear this from me, but..." Once you
figure out what people are unwilling to talk about openly, dig deeper to
understand why and foster more faith in safe, open conversation.

What are we afraid to lose? What do we stand to gain?
Risk aversion often stems from a fear of loss so identify which stakes people
feel the need to protect. Look at the true cost of loss and if there are ways to
prevent it or balance it out. Give people a reason to believe in the potential
benefits of change.

Who is responsible?
If responsibility is concentrated with one person or group, then the stakes
may feel unreasonably high. Consider ways to spread responsibility and
diffuse fear through shared accountability. Foster confidence through
collaboration.

How is risk rewarded or punished?
Most people can offer a cautionary tale about why not to do something. Look
for examples of how risk has been disciplined in the past and how that might
be influencing current ways of thinking. Often people and conditions change,
but the fear remains. Balance stories of tragedy with stories of triumph.

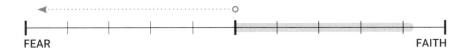

FEAR   FAITH

Striking the Balance: How to Remedy too much Faith

If Faith is exerting too much pull, dial down the Courage and consider the consequences (both intended and unintended) of your efforts. Innovation requires risk. The key to progress is to balance the creative tension between Fear of change with Faith in your capabilities to creatively address the consequences of new ways of working.

How might we apply Courage to bring integrity to our Faith?
We can use the same questions as before to help diagnose where some Fear could help:

What are we afraid to talk about?
If things feel risky, people probably have concerns that they are not voicing. Make sure there is a safe space for expressing doubts and uncertainties about leaps of faith. Use these conversations to surface fears and explore scenarios.

What are we afraid to lose? What do we stand to gain?
Don't lose sight of what already is when pursuing what could be. Identify the opportunity costs of taking risks and discuss the trade offs. Take the time to assess advantages and disadvantages of a risk. Determine ways to protect vulnerabilities.

Who is responsible?
Risk affection may stem from a lack of awareness about consequences or direct responsibility for efforts and outcomes. Identify who the stakeholders are and how they are impacted (directly or indirectly) by risks.

How is risk rewarded or punished?
It's easy to focus on epic tales of heroic success when we want to justify a big risk. Tales of catastrophe can be equally inspiring and educational. Balance the allure of wild success with honest conversations about the potential costs of failure.

THE SOURCE OF TENSION IS: ASSESSMENT

Assessment is related to how efforts and outcomes are measured; belief that what is measured will grow. Ability to learn from experience and transfer learning to others.

It responds to the question "What to Measure?"

Tension related to assessment is created by the opposing forces of Failure and Fuel. Failure is not better than the Fuel. Fuel is not better than Failure. They are both valuable when pursuing innovative solutions. They can also be difficult to balance so it is valuable to diagnose which Force may be exerting too much influence on a process, project or individual and remedy that imbalance with an **Evolution** mindset.

▶ Evolution is gradual and constant development from a simple state into a more complex state.

Evolution involves the belief that things today are impacted by what happened in the past. It also means that it is possible to impact the future with today's choices and actions. As an approach or mindset, evolution requires a desire to deliberately contribute to future development. This is done through the generation and application of insights about past efforts.

If we are not deliberate in how we learn and progress, we leave our development up to chance. To embrace our evolution, as individuals and teams and organizations, we must be willing to succeed and fail. And no matter the outcomes, we must be prepared to learn and grow.

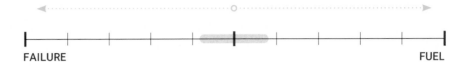

FAILURE   FUEL

Assessment provides input and feedback that shapes growth. When there is very little assessment happening it means not enough people are asking and answering the question "What to measure?". It signals that there is not enough information available to impact deliberate development. It means that it's time to learn how to learn.

Apply an Evolution mindset to increase the impact of assessment.

Learning is not just about collecting data. It involves analysis of information, synthesis into insights and identification of actions to continue or change in the future. There are essentially two ways to learn from an experience: reflect on it while it is happening or reflect on it afterwards.

Learning in the moment may be associated with the force of Fuel because it happens quickly. Insights can be immediately applied to efforts to determine if they are valuable. The Failure force tends to value retrospective learning that occurs after an effort is complete so that the results can be factored into the assessment. To expand the impact of assessment and get deliberate about evolving, it's important to increase both approaches to learning.

The questions below are starting points to trigger some reflection and help you think about the different ways that you can use assessment to deliberately evolve yourself, situation, team, organization, etc.

. . . .

What can we learn from?

What sources of information are already available to you?

Consider what kind of existing data you can refer to as a starting point. Look for quantitative metrics that provides a big picture view. Also seek out more qualitative information that gives substance and context to the numbers. Consider past projects and/or processes.

Who can we learn from?
Who are the gurus in your midst?

You are surrounded by wisdom, it is yours for the asking. So ask for it! Talk to internal people like those who have long tenure with the organization, product or team and can share lessons. Talk to new people who can provide a fresh, unbiased take or inspiration from the outside. Look outside of the organization for insights about the industry, competition or relevant trends.

What have we done well or not?
What can you learn from successes and failures?

Take a look at the projects and people that are considered successful. There may be lessons that apply to other initiatives. Review projects or people that were considered failures. Again, there are lots of great lessons that can be generated about what to avoid, what to try, what to troubleshoot, etc.

How might we measure during and after?
What can you start measuring and learning from?

Remember the two types of learning. Explore ways to reflect on processes and projects while you are in the middle of them and at the conclusion. Consider different ways to assess people, performance, progress towards goals, etc. Imagine how to adjust or adapt if necessary.

How might we curate and communicate our learning?
What are some ways that you can make insights easy to find and share?

Lessons are great, they are even better when they can be shared with others and easily referenced. Reduce the risk of redundancy and having to learn hard lessons repeatedly by generating tools or methods for making learning a shared experience. This is especially helpful when people transition into or out of projects, roles and teams.

. . . .

Improve Integrity: How to Balance

Apply an Evolution mindset to increase the integrity of assessment.
Embracing the potential to shape an evolutionary transformation from simple
to complex helps balance the opposing forces of Failure and Fuel. When
these forces are in equilibrium it means you are getting the best of both
worlds and leveraging diverse strengths. Balance signifies integrity.

FAILURE   FUEL

Striking the Balance: How to Remedy too much Failure

When we are overburdened by a good/bad Failure paradigm that focuses too
much on the outcomes and not enough on the process, it's helpful to pause
and consider how current efforts are contributing to our Evolution. We can
ask ourselves what lessons we are learning that will help us grow into a more
complex and capable organization, team or individual.

How might we apply Evolution to bring integrity to our Failure?
Some questions to ask that help diagnose where some Fuel could help:

What can we learn from our failures?
There is always something valuable to learn when things don't quite go the
way we hope or expect. Especially if we want to avoid similar outcomes in
the future. Celebrate surprises and search for lessons in the unintended
consequences of your actions.

In what ways might we empower individuals or teams to assess and adjust?
In most situations, assessment is power. The people who measure and track
results get to determine what is worthy of attention and the consequences
for meeting goals (or not). To improve integrity of assessment, encourage
teams and individuals to develop their own systems for assessing activities
and acting on that information. Then encourage them to share their findings.

How might we promote and support learning agility?
In order too balance a focus on outcomes-based assessment, it may help
to explore ways to promote more learning-in-the-moment. Give people
permission to act on these "smaller" learnings by making immediately
changes. Encourage dissemination of these lessons so they can be
integrated in a widespread way.

FAILURE   FUEL

Striking the Balance: How to Remedy too much Fuel

When we are too caught up in learning new things and accepting everything
as a success, we need to turn down the speed of Evolution. This will provide
time and space to get clear about our goals and how to move deliberately
and strategically towards them. We can balance a love of learning with
appreciation for achievement.

How might we apply Evolution to bring integrity to our Fuel?
Some questions to ask that help diagnose where some Failure could help:

What strategic goals or initiatives are we pursuing right now?
Make sure that current efforts map back to strategic goals. Identify how
specific efforts or activities support a bigger mission or purpose. If they
don't, they may need to be reconsidered.

How might we track progress to improve our understanding?
It is helpful to ensure that current efforts are being documented in a format
that makes them viable sources for reflection and learning. If someone
looked back at the project, would they understand why decisions were made
and how they impacted the outcomes?

Who is responsible for what? Is there accountability?
Making deliberate progress towards goals requires clarity about roles and
responsibility. To avoid distractions, find ways to build in accountability and
reflect on what is working or not.

What lessons are we applying?
Pursuit of new opportunities can be alluring. Balance the call of the novel
with an earnest assessment of past efforts. Take the time to explicitly
identify lessons that can be applied to new ventures.

THE SOURCE OF TENSION IS: PACE OF CHANGE

Pace of change is related to the rate of speed at which elements of a system can undergo change and adaptation given the information that is available at the time.

It responds to the question "When to Change?"

Tension related to the pace of change is created by the opposing forces of Frozen and Fast. Frozen is not better than Fast. Fast is not better than Frozen. They are both valuable when pursuing innovative solutions. They can also be difficult to balance so it is valuable to diagnose which Force may be exerting too much influence on a process, project or individual and remedy that imbalance with **Experimentation**.

► Experimentation is a discovery
process that includes iterative
cycles of action and reflection.

Innovation requires a willingness to experiment: to try in the face of
uncertainty and to learn from that trial. It also requires a willingness to fail,
i.e. to experience unintended outcomes from our efforts so that we can
improve our understanding and reduce the uncertainty.

Although the concept of experiments may conjure up images of scientists
in lab coats and rigorous methods, a research orientation doesn't have to be
so formal and sterile. An experimentation mindset is really about systematic
inquiry, i.e. a deliberately designed effort to learn from both the process and
product of an activity. This can happen at various speeds.

Increase Impact: How to Stretch

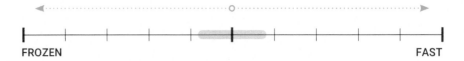

FROZEN   FAST

If we aren't changing, then we aren't evolving. When there is no pace of change that means that change is not happening at all or only when required by outside influences. When an organization, team or individual is not being responsive to internal and external influences it risks becoming irrelevant.

Apply an Experimentation mindset to increase the impact of the pace of change.

Deliberate transformation can be fast or slow, and should be the result of understanding. To increase the impact of the pace of change means to use experimentation to inspire relevant and valuable change. Experimentation is rooted in the scientific method and includes basic steps: observation, questioning, hypothesizing, testing, analyzing and concluding. The entire cycle (and the steps within it) can be applied with various velocities.

The questions below are starting points to help you think about the kind of experimentation that is relevant for your situation, team, organization, etc.

. . . .

What are we observing?

What are you looking at that may inspire experiments?

People are constantly consuming information in many forms so there are likely plenty of things to inspire thinking about opportunities for change. Consider looking at people (internal and external), processes, products and services and the environment (physical, social, cultural, political, etc.

What questions do we have?

Are these observations raising any questions about your work?

Given the things that are happening, think about what inspires more curiosity. Identify areas to dig deeper into, whether they seem immediately relevant or not. Sometimes what seems like a tangent can prove to be quite relevant.

What assumptions do we have?

How are your observations inspiring hypotheses?

Everyone has assumptions about the past, about the present and about the future. Consider what conclusions you are drawing about the information before you. IS there anything that should questioned or more deeply understood?

How might we test our assumptions?

What kinds of experiments can you design to test your hypotheses?

There are lots of tools for testing and lots of ways to gather information that will reveal new opportunities and inform decisions. Think about what kind of stimulus you can make (i.e. prototypes, models, etc.) that will make it possible to solicit feedback. Consider different modes of collecting data different types of data.

How might we assess the outcomes of our tests?

What will you do with the data you collect?

It's helpful to ask this question before you conduct an actual experiment because it forces you to consider what you will do with the data you collect during your experiment. Explore methods to use for analysis of data and how they might generate actionable insights. Consider the audience for the results and how to optimize the format of results to best meet their needs.

How might we act on information and communicate that?

What kind of change is desirable? How will you share?

The purpose of an experiment is to test a hypothesis and arrive at a conclusion, so what's the conclusion? Ideally your efforts will produce recommendations for some sort of action or choice or change, be it big or small. Are you accepting or rejecting the hypothesis? It's possible that the results indicate there is no need to change, that the status quo is just fine.

. . . .

Improve Integrity: How to Balance

Use Experimentation to increase the integrity of the pace of change.
The Experimentation mindset requires both action and reflection. Without action there is nothing to learn from and without reflection there is no learning, just motion. Experimentation helps balance the opposing forces of Frozen and Fast. When these forces are in equilibrium it means that you are getting the best of both worlds and leveraging diverse strengths. Balance signifies integrity.

FROZEN   FAST

Striking the Balance: How to Remedy too much Frozen

When we are Frozen we probably spend too much time in reflection and not enough time in action. We come up with additional types of information we believe we need to collect or alternative approaches to analyzing our data. All of this reflection and analysis prevents forward motion and change, keeping us stuck.

To balance the overwhelming force of Frozen, we need to be willing to act and to take risks. We likely need to increase our awareness and sensitivity to the kinds of information out there that might signal a need for change. When faced with opportunities or decisions, we must find comfort in efforts that will generate data to propel us toward more optimal outcomes.

How might we apply Experimentation to bring integrity to our Frozen?
Some questions to ask that help diagnose where some Fast could help:

What do we see that we can act upon now?
Look around for small opportunities and actions that don't require layers of approval to get moving. The act of seeking out new information is a great place to start. Look in unusual places for trends or topics that you may want to put on your radar.

What questions can we answer quickly?
Consider making a nice big list of all the questions that you and others have. Sort the list in terms of what can be answered more quickly. Consider how bigger questions can be broken down into smaller questions for more rapid inquiry.

How might we break down our assumptions into smaller hypotheses?
As with questions, assumptions can also be broken down into smaller, bite-sized pieces. Consider testing hypotheses (at least in a preliminary way) with

smaller sample sizes or with quicker methods that allow you to get feedback about hunches. You can always use lengthier methods later.

In what ways might we conduct some small, quick tests?
Consider the techniques you usually use and if they can be scaled back (i.e. fewer participants, less diversity, less cost). Try thought experiments to answer questions like "How would we test this if we had no budget?" or "What would a startup do to answer this question quickly?"

How might we increase the speed of data analysis?
Sometimes data analysis requires even more time than data collection so think of ways to increase the speed of making meaning from your information. There may be tools for automating analysis or doing it real time. You may want to deploy a team of people to do it in a compressed time frame. Reconsider how deep you really need to go into the data to generate actionable insights. Sometimes skimming the surface reveals provocative patterns.

Are there actions suggested by our data that we can prototype?
If your insights indicate the need for massive change, consider how to break these actions down into smaller steps that can be deployed quickly. Prioritize the most important first steps and create prototypes or pilots that allow you to confirm your results and get more feedback.

FROZEN   FAST

Striking the Balance: How to Remedy too much Fast

When we are moving too Fast, we may lost sight of the reasons for pursuing change. We get caught in the trap of change for the sake of change, because it is exciting and new and exhilarating. We probably need to slow down a bit and make space to reflect on our actions so that we can generate insights and assess the appropriateness of our efforts. We may also need to take the time to ensure that we are communicating our reasons for change to other people who are impacted.

How might we apply Experimentation to bring integrity to our Fast?
Some questions to ask that help diagnose where some Frozen could help:

What is on our radar that we can slow down and observe?
Big shifts and trends often take years to develop. Look for interesting changes happening in big scale, macro ways that may affect you in the long term. If you are focused on details and minutiae, think about how to step back and look at the bigger picture. It can be daunting, but worth it.

What questions do we have that require deep exploration?
The world moves fast, but sometimes impact takes time. A great example is a longevity study that tracks participants from childhood into adulthood. Are there any questions you have today that might take years to fully understand? The time is now to consider them so you can start collecting data or engage someone else in that endeavor.

How might we understand the bigger picture of our many hypotheses?
The allure and benefits of focused, rapid testing can overshadow the value of seeing things in a more systemic, connected way. Explore ways to combine multiple hypotheses to develop more comprehensive theories. Think about ways to dive deeper below the surface to understand the complex nature of the situation.

In what ways might we conduct more in-depth research?
If you are accustomed to rapid turnaround times on testing, slow down a bit to think about what you are learning and how. Are there opportunities to dig deeper or expand your area of focus? Consider other people you might learn from, places you might go to collect information, or techniques that require more time and resources. Take a systemic perspective and explore how things are connected. What would you try to achieve with 6 months, a huge team and an unlimited budget?

How might we spend more time with data analysis?
If you find yourself skimming the surface of data collection and analysis consider taking more time to really get into the information. Deeper analysis of richer data may reveal additional opportunities and increase confidence with decision making. Identify the skeptics in your midst and consider the type of information that is influential for them. Explore assessment methods that are more rigorous or time-consuming.

How might we communicate the implications of our findings?
When you are comfortable acting quickly about the results of your experiments, you risk leaving behind people who don't understand the choices you are making. Take the time to translate your insights (or intuition) into something tangible that provides a compelling justification for change. If it is necessary to move fast, it helps to leave a clear trail for those who may want to trace your footsteps or learn from your efforts.

THE SOURCE OF TENSION IS: AMBIGUITY

Ambiguity is related to tolerance for uncertainty and willingness to proceed with a plan that is likely to change during the course of implementation.

It responds to the question "How to Adapt?"

Tension related to ambiguity is created by the opposing forces of Familiar and Foreign. Familiar is not better than Foreign. Foreign is not better than Familiar. They are both valuable when pursuing innovative solutions. They can also be difficult to balance so it is valuable to diagnose which Force may be exerting too much influence on a process, project or individual and remedy that imbalance with **Curiosity**.

▶ Curiosity is the desire to experience or learn something new.

To exercise curiosity, one must have a genuine interest in seeing something in a new way and the motivation to be impacted or transformed by that experience. Curiosity requires us to open our eyes and our minds to the possibility that things may be different than we think or hope they are.

The world as we know it may actually be quite different than we perceive. As we bring our curiosity to alternative ways of knowing, we may find perspectives that help us navigate what feels unfamiliar. We may find opportunities for new thinking in old ways of doing and being. Curiosity is a deliberate choice to seek and find new meaning.

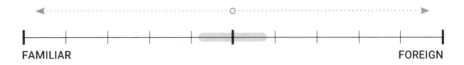

Increase Impact: How to Stretch

FAMILIAR   FOREIGN

Much as we may like to believe that we can predict the future and set reasonable expectations, uncertainty is one of the most certain things there is. Ambiguity is about not knowing for sure what will happen, and being willing to proceed anyway. When the span of ambiguity is small it likely means that we are not having honest conversations about our certitude. To increase the impact of ambiguity means to clarify what we think may happen and how we are prepared to respond.

Apply Curiosity mindset to increase the impact of ambiguity.

Use Curiosity to explore how to navigate ambiguity as you move forward. Be curious about patterns and consistencies from past efforts or similar situations. These can help reduce uncertainty and increase understanding of what to expect. Explore assumptions. It can be easier to dive into the unknown if there is some sense of what you might find there. Be willing to learn something new and be transformed by that understanding.

The questions below are starting points to help you think about how tolerance for uncertainty impacts efforts in your situation, team, organization, etc.

. . . .

What is changing? What isn't? Why?

What is going on right now that we need to consider as we proceed?

Explore what changes are currently underway and what might be on the horizon. These might be internal changes related to resources, people, tools, etc. You can also consider big environmental impacts like politics, policies, technology, society, environment, economy, etc. It's also worth looking at what's not changing and consider why that is. Generating scenarios or stories makes uncertainty feel a little more tangible.

How might we prepare for uncertainty?
What are some ways that we might respond to changes that arise?

It's hard to imagine preparing for things that you aren't sure will happen, but it's possible. Use scenarios of things that may play out in the future to explore how you would respond. What would disaster preparedness look like for your project, product, team, etc.?

How flexible/firm is the plan?
Where might we be more willing and able to adapt or not?

Examine ways that your plan or process can be more or less rigid. Think about removing redundancy, layers, activities or unnecessary communication. Consider how to reorganize or optimize steps. Try to balance the flexible and firm so that there is clarity of what is expected as well as space to adapt to inevitable changes.

What are others doing to adapt to uncertainty?
How are others facing and responding to changes that impact their efforts?

Look for examples that are nearby and familiar (i.e. within your own team, organization, industry, region, etc.) Seek out examples that feel unfamiliar (i.e. within adjacent or unrelated industries, cutting edge companies, different teams, regions or countries with whom you feel you have little in common, etc.) The point is to get curious about what others are doing and see if their familiar or foreign approaches can inspire new ideas or help reduce feelings of uncertainty.

· ·

Improve Integrity: How to Balance

Apply a Curiosity mindset to increase the integrity of Ambiguity.
Curiosity about what is known and unknown helps us navigate ambiguity and manage the tension between the Familiar and the Foreign. Depending on which Force is pulling us out of balance we have to apply Curiosity in different ways. When these forces are in equilibrium it means we are getting the best of both worlds and leveraging diverse strengths. Balance signifies integrity.

FAMILIAR   FOREIGN

Striking the Balance: How to Remedy too much Familiar

When the Familiar overly influences us, turn up the Curiosity and look for opportunities in new places with new people and/or processes. As we apply curiosity to generate scenarios of what could happen and how to respond, we can temper our need for certainty with curiosity about what might be possible. Curiosity provides insight and inspiration from unusual sources. When Familiar ways no longer produce the results we desire, it's time to embrace the unknown.

How might we apply Curiosity to bring integrity to our Familiar?
Some questions to ask that help diagnose where some Foreign could help:

Who are the skeptics and what are they saying?
When things are too familiar it likely means you are talking to people who see things the way you do. Expand your horizons. Talk to strangers, especially those who don't believe what you do. Seek out dissenting opinions and divergent points of view. Allow yourself to consider the problems and solutions from different perspectives.

How are others responding to changes?
You already know quite well how you would approach the problem. Remedy a reliance on tradition by considering how "not you" would approach the situation. Think about inspiring people or innovative organizations that are unrelated to your field. You can even use fictional characters. Ask yourself, given the challenge at hand, "What would ___ do?" and come up with many possible answers.

What might be all the things we can prepare for?
The world is always changing. Rather than fear it, embrace it and prepare for it. Try to improve current solutions by projecting into the future. Identify all of the possible events or changes that could impact your efforts. Once you have this list, get creative about how to respond. Be inspired by the unknown and seek novelty in your solutions.

What if we had to... ?
Play games that expand thinking beyond the usual and comfortable. Ask yourself how you might solve the very same problem less money, resources, time, etc. What if you had half the resource or a third or even less? What would you do if an essential element, like equipment or technology or a method, were no longer available? Imagine having to start from scratch. What if you didn't have any of the current resources, knowledge, access, etc.? Try to think like an entrepreneur who is trying to break into the market with limited resources and big ideas.

What are the dumb questions?
When we are mired in the familiar, we tend to (unknowingly) take things for granted. Break out of this autopilot thinking by engaging some folks who are not familiar with the project, process, industry, etc. Give them a very high level description of the opportunity or task and invite them to ask all the questions they want. Don't worry about answering their questions, or making sure they understand things as well as the experts. Just listen and let the questions provoke new thinking.

FAMILIAR   FOREIGN

Striking the Balance: How to Remedy too much Foreign

If we are overly enamored by the Foreign, we can direct our Curiosity towards what we already have around us and explore existing resources through a different lens. Curiosity helps us to find something comfortable and familiar in the strange or to find something strange and unusual in the familiar. Balancing a heavy influence of the Foreign is about acknowledging its connections and contributions to Familiar elements.

How might we increase Curiosity to bring integrity to our Foreign?
Some questions to ask that help diagnose where some Familiar could help:

How might we communicate our efforts?
The Foreign only feels that way the when we experience it for the first time.
The more exposure we have to something unusual, the more comfortable
we become with it. Look for ways to document and communicate new
approaches and insights so they feel less foreign to others. Consider
having a dedicated team "translator" who is responsible for communicating
progress in a language that feel familiar to the rest of the organization.

How do our efforts connect to strategic goals, past efforts, etc?
Explore ways to connect unusual methods to strategic objectives. It's easier
for people to step into unfamiliar territory if there is a clear line of sight
between an activity and a potential outcome that serves bigger goals. It may
also be possible to establish a connection with past projects or demonstrate
how a new approach builds on previous efforts and moves them forward.

What can we systematize or replicate?
Point your curiosity in the direction of those who may wish to follow in your
footsteps. Think about what they would need to know or do to replicate your
approach. It's okay if you don't want to do something the same way twice.
Just leave a trail so someone else can learn from what you've done. Consider
how novel methods can be documented so they can be shared, replicated
and improved. This might be the first time, but it doesn't have to be the last.

How might we leverage what's familiar?
When you are embarking on a journey filled with uncertainty, identify which
elements feel familiar. Try to integrate things that provide comfort in times
of turbulence. You might use traditional terms and metaphors to describe
unusual processes or apply standard metrics to measure progress. Use
stories to soothe concerns, perhaps drawing from adjacent industries or
other contexts where your approach has worked well.

How might we take some baby steps?
If it's too hard to make big sweeping changes and adopt completely new
ways of doing, start with baby steps. Sometimes it takes a tiny effort
everyday to make a big shift over time. Balance the heavy pull of the Familiar
by looking for little ways to introduce novel thinking and methods that pull
in the other direction. Think strategically about who to engage and what to
try. Document your efforts and spread the word. The more people hear about
something, the less unusual it seems.

THE SOURCE OF TENSION IS: PLAYING FIELD

Playing Field is about understanding key stakeholders who impact and are impacted, awareness of context and landscape that shapes decision making.

It responds to the question "Who Matters?"

Tension related to the playing field is created by the opposing forces of Fierce and Friends. Fierce is not better than Friends. Friends is not better than Fierce. They are both valuable when pursuing innovative solutions. They can also be difficult to balance so it is valuable to diagnose which Force may be exerting too much influence on a process, project or individual and remedy that imbalance with **Connection**.

▶ Connection is the intentional relationship between two or more entities.

In order to connect, we must be willing to associate unique things, to link them together in a way that is mutually beneficial. With connection we are able to bring things closer to each other to understand the relationship between them. With that proximity we can explore ways to engage and link and unite and empower. We can also identify ways to divide, distinguish, exclude and overpower.

Through connection we learn to find balance so that each entity has the potential to survive and thrive. We are able to search for the similarities that unite us as well as differences that divide us. Both will reveal opportunities to grow in unique ways. Through connection we must also be willing to explore our boundaries in order to create distinction from one another.

Increase Impact: How to Stretch

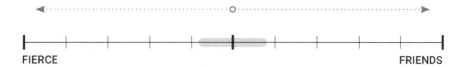

FIERCE   FRIENDS

The Playing Field provides a context for identifying opportunities and making decisions. When the span is small, it means that there is not much awareness about the landscape. If no one is asking "Who matters?" then it's possible that everyone matters or no one does. To increase the impact of the playing field means to get intentional about the relationships that shape actions and experiences.

Apply a Connection mindset to increase the impact of the playing field.

Use Connection to understand the ecosystem of different stakeholders and how they relate to each other (or not). This means giving thoughtful consideration to different groups, organizations and people and looking at their relationships to each other; how they are, or could be, connected. Consider who you want to draw closer. It also means thinking about who (or what) you need to distance yourself from in order to distinguish yourself.

The questions below are starting points to help you think about the kind of relationships that are relevant for your situation, team, organization, etc.

What is the game?
What problems are we trying to solve?

Think about the basics first. What is the name of the game? In other words, what is the purpose of the individual team, organization, etc? This can be a statement about "why I/we are doing this." Get clear about motivations, intentions, passions and goals. Clarify the problems that you are trying to solve and why that is important.

What are the rules?

How do things typically play out in this context, situation, team, industry?

Identify the guidelines for your work or your market. These may be explicit, clearly stated policies or legally binding rules. They may be implicit, unspoken assumptions and norms about "how things are supposed to be done around here". Consider how the rules affect work processes, including how decisions are made and opportunities are prioritized. Are the rules changing? Is there a reason you might want them to change? How might you impact the rules?

Who are the players?

Who are the different stakeholders? What are their relationships to each other?

A stakeholder is anyone that is concerned with, or impacted by, your efforts. A stakeholder can be an individual or a group. A stakeholder can have a primary, direct connection (i.e. someone on the team or a customer) or a secondary, indirect connection (i.e. a distributor or competitor). As you consider the landscape of stakeholders include competitors, alliances, partners and customers. You can also think about other organizations that serve your customer's needs in similar, different, or unrelated ways. Identify people who may be underserved or have unmet needs that you are qualified to satisfy. Look for potential partners and relationships that can benefit many parties.

What is the prize?

What does it mean to win? How is success measured or achieved?

Think of ways to reframe success. Maybe it isn't about beating out the competition, maybe it's about complementing their capabilities or even improving their offering by providing something that they can't and you can. Leverage your unique capabilities to find new ways to shine with the people who matter.

Improve Integrity: How to Balance

Apply a Connection mindset to increase the integrity of the playing field.
Connection with other people helps us balance the tension between feeling
Fierce and feeling like Friends. Depending on which Force is pulling us
out of balance we have to apply Connection in different ways. When these
forces are in equilibrium it means we are getting the best of both worlds and
leveraging diverse strengths. Balance signifies integrity.

FIERCE   FRIENDS

Striking the Balance: How to Remedy too much Fierce

Connection allows us to balance the exclusivity of Fierce competition with
the unifying potential of Friendship. When the force of competition is too
much, we can increase Connection through efforts to understand others and
intentionally develop nourishing relationships with those we fear or fight.

In lieu of a battle, we can adopt a stance of appreciation. If we consider the
value of our "opponents" we might learn from them instead of try to destroy
them. When we temper our ferocious behavior with Connection, we can
transform win-lose situations into opportunities for a win-win.

How might we apply Connection to bring integrity to our Fierce?
Some questions to ask that help diagnose where some Friends could help:

What problems are we trying to solve and why?
To turn up the Friends force, think about connecting more with people
(your team, your clients, your vendors, your competitors). Expand your
understanding of the problems that you are solving by finding out how
others experience those problems and what consequences result from
your solutions. Are there other related problems to address? Are there new
problems that you hadn't thought of that you might try to solve? How can you
seek solutions that benefit as many stakeholders as possible?

What can and should change about how we work?
Think about what is not working with the way things currently work. If the
environment is toxic or people are unhappy, figure out why that is happening
and address it. You may have to change the rules of the game. Be willing to
challenge assumptions and explore alternative ways of working. The goal is
to improve the experience for as many people as possible, to treat each other
as friends.

How might we reframe our relationships?
Think about all the stakeholders. Focus specifically on the ones (internal
or external) with whom you have the strongest competitive orientation.
Appreciate the competition by identifying what they do really well and why
that is valuable. What can you learn from that? What might be the benefits of
strengthening your relationship with them? Ask your self about who else you
could befriend, partner with, treat better, etc. and why that might generate
valuable for multiple parties.

How might we reframe our goals to be more beneficial to more people?
Imagine that you have competition whatsoever. Imagine that "winning" is
guaranteed. How might that change the way you think about your goals or
efforts? Consider how the drive to fiercely compete and win may harshly
impact the people involved. Explore how to approach problems and deliver
solutions in ways that produce a "win-win-win" where everyone involved
benefits and feels valued in the experience. What might that look like?

FIERCE   FRIENDS

Striking the Balance: How to Remedy too much Friends

If our Friendly orientation threatens our survival, we can turn down the
Connection to build up boundaries. We may need to distinguish ourselves
and improve our capacity to make tough decisions that put or own interests
first. A Connection mindset enables us to increase or decrease the
interdependent nature of our relationships in a way that boosts the benefits
for all.

How might we apply Connection to bring integrity to our Friends?
Some questions to ask that help diagnose where some Fierce could help:

What game do we really want to play?
It can be easy to slide into a place of comfortable complacency where no
one challenges choices and everyone avoids disruptive change. Maybe it's
time to take a hard look at your goals and determine which problems you
most want to solve and which solutions you want to provide to whom. Once
you have clarity about that, assess your current situation to determine if you
have the resources and people you need to meet those goals. If not, it's time
to make some changes.

How does our performance compare with others?
Look at your rivals to understand what they are doing well and how your performance measures up. It's not always easy, but one healthy way to balance out a lack of accountability is to connect your efforts to your competition through comparison. Don't let personal relationships get in the way of objective assessments that yield insights for how to improve performance.

Who is taking advantage of our goodwill?
If the force of Friends is too strong then there's a strong likelihood that someone is profiting from your generous spirit. They may not be intentionally malicious, but they are benefiting at your expense. Identify where deference to personal relationships is hindering performance or progress. Establish clear boundaries. Fortify your defenses against those who manipulate situations in their favor and at your expense.

Why aren't we winning?
Critically assess your situation and identify strengths and weaknesses of your efforts compared to others. Get more competitive. Identify where you are avoiding competition and explore what is holding you back. Figure out what it takes to win over people, customers, leaders, markets, etc. and generate a plan to do it. To compete means to fight for what you believe. Be prepared to lose friends along the way but don't compromise your integrity.

This section described the innovation facilitator's mindset and how it can be applied to address the six tensions of transformation.

Innovation is difficult because change creates tension. Tension is a byproduct of how people relate to each other through the processes of work. When faced with transformation, people may resist anything they perceive as a threat to their values and preferences.

The innovation facilitator must model attitudes and behaviors that help people to navigate these tensions and find ways to meet in the middle. This means demonstrating:

Empathy
The ability to understand the experience of another, to walk in someone else's shoes and see the world as they do.

Courage
Having the heart to face that which we fear.

Evolution
Gradual and constant development from a simple state into a more complex state.

Experimentation
A discovery process that includes iterative cycles of action and reflection.

Curiosity
The desire to experience or learn something new.

Connection
The intentional relationship between two or more entities.

No matter what tools or techniques we use to innovate, we will face challenges as people stretch into new ways of thinking and doing. When we use these projects as opportunities to help people bring the best of themselves to the work and appreciate the diversity of what others can offer, it is possible that our efforts can produce more than innovative outcomes. They can also produce innovative people who understand how to diagnose tensions that arise and remedy them together.

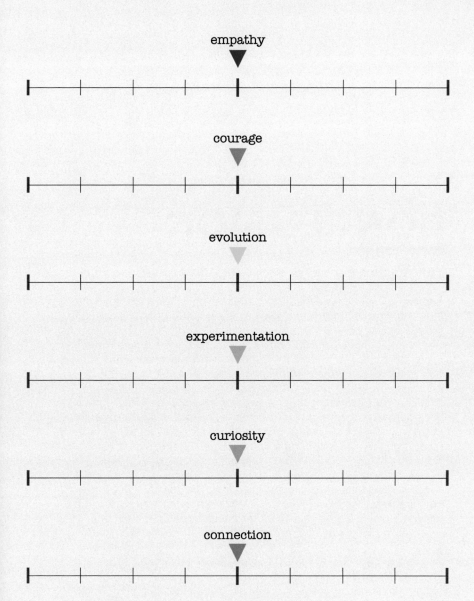

CONCLUSION

Innovation can be pretty f-ing hard.

Anytime we set out to change, to transform an existing situation into a preferred one, our efforts are likely to generate tension. The fundamental tension occurs between Business-As-Usual (BAU), the standard comfortable way of doing things, and a Creativity Sustaining Atmosphere (CSA), an exploratory space of imagination and possibility. The tension is a result of opposing forces pulling in opposite directions.

This core tension manifests across the different dimensions outlined in this book. The six tensions of transformation include knowledge, risk, assessment, pace of change, ambiguity, and the playing field. For each dimension there are paradigms of thinking and doing that influence how work gets done.

These tensions are systemic, they occur within individuals, teams and organizations. Diagnosing the source of tension is the first step in understanding why things may be feeling so difficult. It's also the first step in identifying how to facilitate innovation efforts.

We have to be willing to look at the tension, to love it even. Tension itself is good and ideally it is really strong. Creative tension means people are bringing their very best thinking and skills to the task at hand. Once we know what the tension is, we can learn to navigate it when we bring opposing forces together.

Assessing tension involves looking at the intensity of the influences pulling in different directions (i.e. the impact) and how strong those forces are. Ideally they are both exerting a strong influence. It's also important to assess the balance between the two forces, i.e. the integrity of influence from both forces. If one force is exerting too much power it leads to dissonance and disillusionment.

For each of the six tensions there is a corresponding attitude or behavior that can be used to address the lack of impact or integrity. These six remedies collectively represent the innovation facilitator's mindset, i.e. a way of thinking and doing that can help innovators to ease the tensions and bring out the best of their people and their teams.

Knowledge
empathy
▼

BAU   CSA

FACTS   FEELINGS

Risk
courage
▼

BAU   CSA

FEAR   FAITH

Assessment
evolution
▼

BAU   CSA

FAILURE   FUEL

Pace of Change
experimentation
▼

BAU   CSA

FROZEN   FAST

Ambiguity
curiosity
▼

BAU   CSA

FAMILIAR   FOREIGN

Playing Field
connection
▼

BAU   CSA

FIERCE   FRIENDS

Tension is good. It means that there are strong forces at play and great expertise that can be applied to the challenge. To balance tensions doesn't mean to minimize or destroy the differences. Rather, it means to foster understanding and awareness so that it is easier for people to meet in the middle. This is the task of the innovation facilitator—to transform the tension into innovation.

We need tension to do our best work. We need to embrace our strengths and expertise and preferences and then be willing to consider the incredible value of the absolute opposite. If it weren't for the opposing forces, we probably wouldn't get to do what we most love to do. We need each other.

Breakthrough innovation is most likely to occur when people bring the best of themselves to the task, and make space for others to bring alternative ways of thinking and doing.

Sure, it will be f-ing hard. Anything worthwhile is.

Made in the USA
San Bernardino, CA
20 August 2016